POETIC GEMS

D1329041

POETIC GEMS

William McGonagall

Poet and Tragedian

DUCKWORTH

Second impression 1992
First published in this edition 1989

Gerald Duckworth & Co Ltd
The Old Piano Factory
48 Hoxton Square, London N1 6PB

ISBN 0 7156 2299 4

Typeset by Elanders Computer Assisted
Typesetting Systems, Inverness
and printed and bound in Great Britain by
Redwood Press Limited, Melksham, Wiltshire

CONTENTS

FOREWORD

by Billy Connolly

WILLIAM TOPAZ McGONAGALL was many things to many people: the Prince of Doggerel, a great writer of bad verse, a funny wee man, a laugh, a joke, an idjit. He was portrayed as a wee man with a red beard in a kilt too big for him.

To himself he was the complete artiste: tragedian, poet, composer of fine songs and music, playwright, entertainer. He believed it was his duty to perform his wares and skills. Not even when his poor demented wife was forced to work in the laundry of an asylum in Dundee, and pleaded for him to return to the hand-loom weaving, would he ever consider working in any other trade, except that which The Muse had blessed or cursed him with.

The Muse didn't supply him with a sense of humour when she gave him his other skills. He didn't laugh when they shouted abuse in the streets at him, nor when the landlords tipped the dregs of beer over him when he was reciting in their pubs. They hid his hat and left it cut up in pieces. The local press were always having a go when they ran out of something to sneer at. A student wrote to him professing to be the Poet Laureate of Burmah at the court of King Theebaw and saying that from that day forth he might be called 'Sir William Topaz McGonagall, knight of the white Elephant'. The students invited him to entertain them, and then sneered and laughed at him. He performed in pubs, blacksmith's shops, church halls, theatres, class-rooms, even in a circus.

To McGonagall it made no difference. The world was a circus – a circus of cruel people whose only pleasure in life seemed to be to abuse others worse off than themselves. He lived in abject poverty. When he did a tour of Fife he came back with less than when he began his trip. Local dignitaries tried to stop him in his crusade, because they felt he gave a poor image of the culture of Dundee. Time after time he warned Dundee that if the city didn't treat him better he would seek his fortune elsewhere. He emigrated to New York and then to London and Glasgow, which he quite liked. They even treated him with respect, but it wasn't home, so he returned to Dundee.

Sir William Topaz McGonagall considered himself to be the finest exponent of Shakespeare in the world – bar one man, but he lived in London, so that didn't count. He considered himself, above all else, a genius, and it was the world's failing not to recognise him.

Perhaps genius is the relentless pursuit of one's imagining. If so, Sir William Topaz McGonagall was truly a genius. He remained, until his dying breath, a gentleman.

PREFACE

MY DEARLY BELOVED READERS, — I will begin with giving an account of my experiences amongst the publicans. Well, I must say that the first man who threw peas at me was a publican, while I was giving an entertainment to a few of my admirers in a public-house in a certain little village not far from Dundee; but, my dear friends, I wish it to be understood that the publican who threw the peas at me was not the landlord of the public-house, he was one of the party who came to hear me give my entertainment. Well, my dear readers, it was while I was singing my own song, "The Rattling Boy from Dublin Town," that he threw the peas at me. You must understand that the Rattling Boy was courting a lass called Biddy Brown, and the Rattling Boy chanced to meet his Biddy one night in company with another lad called Barney Magee, which, of course, he did not like to see, and he told Biddy he considered it too bad for her to be going about with another lad, and he would bid her good-bye for being untrue to him. Then Barney Magee told the Rattling Boy that Biddy Brown was his ass, and that he could easily find another — and come and have a glass, and be friends. But the Rattling Boy told Barney Magee to give his glass of strong drink to the devil! meaning, I suppose, it was only fit for devils to make use of, not for God's creatures. Because, my friends, too often has strong drink been the cause of seducing many a beautiful young woman away from her true lover, and from her parents also, by a false seducer, which, no doubt, the Rattling Boy considered Barney Magee to be. Therefore, my dear friends, the reason, I think, for the publican throwing the peas at me is because I say,

9

to the devil with your glass, in my song, "The Rattling Boy from Dublin," and he, no doubt, considered it had a teetotal tendency about it, and, for that reason, he had felt angry, and had thrown the peas at me.

My dear readers, my next adventure was as follows: — During the Blue Ribbon Army movement in Dundee, and on the holiday week of the New-year, I was taken into a public-house by a party of my friends and admirers, and requested to give them an entertainment, for which I was to be remunerated by them. Well, my friends, after the party had got a little refreshment, and myself along with the rest, they proposed that I should give them a little entertainment, which I most willingly consented to do, knowing I would be remunerated by the company for so doing, which was the case; the money I received from them I remember amounted to four shillings and sixpence. All had gone on as smoothly as a marriage bell, and every one of the party seemed to be highly delighted with the entertainment I had given them. Of course, you all ought to know that while singing a good song, or giving a good recitation, it helps to arrest the company's attention from the drink; yes! in many cases it does, my friends. Such, at least, was the case with me — at least the publican thought so — for — what do you think? — he devised a plan to bring my entertainment to an end abruptly, and the plan was, he told the waiter to throw a wet towel at me, which, of course, the waiter did, as he was told, and I received the wet towel, full force, in the face, which staggered me no doubt, and had the desired effect of putting an end to me giving any more entertainments in his house. But, of course, the company I had been entertaining felt angry with the publican for being guilty of such a base action towards me, and I felt indignant myself, my friends, and accordingly I left the company I had been entertaining and bade them good-bye. My dear friends, a publican is a creature that would wish to decoy all the money out of the people's pockets that enter his house; he does not want them to give any of their money away for an intellectual entertainment. No, no! by no means; give it all to him, and crush out entertainments altogether, thereby he would make more money if he could only do so. My dear friends, if there were more theatres in society than public-houses, it would be a much better world to live in, at least more moral; and oh! my dear friends, be advised by me. Give your money to the baker, and the butcher, also the shoemaker and the clothier, and shun the publicans; give them no money at all, for this sufficient reason, they would most willingly deprive us of all moral entertainment if we would be as silly as to allow them. They would wish us to think only about what sort of strong drink we should make use of, and to place our affections on that only, and give the most of our earnings to them; no matter whether your families starve or not, or go naked or shoeless; they care not, so as their own families are well clothed from the cold, and well fed. My dear friends, I most sincerely entreat of you to shun the publicans as you would shun the devil, because nothing good can emanate from indulging in strong drink, but only that which is evil. Turn ye, turn ye! why be a slave to the bottle? Turn to God, and He will save you.

I hope the day is near at hand,
When strong drink will be banished from our
    land.

11

I remember a certain publican in the city that always pretended to have a great regard for me. Well, as I chanced to be passing by his door one day he was standing in the doorway, and he called on me to come inside, and, as he had been in the habit of buying my poetry, he asked me if I was getting on well, and, of course, I told him the truth, that I was not getting on very well, that I had nothing to do, nor I had not been doing anything for three weeks past, and, worse than all, I had no poetry to sell. Then he said that was a very bad job, and that he was very sorry to hear it, and he asked me how much I would take to give an entertainment in his large back-room, and I told him the least I would take would be five shillings. Oh! very well, he replied I will invite some of my friends and acquaintances for Friday night first, and mind, you will have to be here at seven o'clock punctual to time, so as not to keep the company waiting. So I told him I would remember the time, and thanked him for his kindness, and bade him good-bye. Well, when Friday came, I was there punctually at seven o'clock, and, when I arrived, he told me I was just in time, and that there was a goodly company gathered to hear me. So he bade me go ben to the big room, and that he would be ben himself — as I supposed more to look after the money than to hear me give my entertainment. Well, my readers, when I made my appearance before the company I was greeted with applause, and they told me they had met together for the evening to hear me give my entertainment. Then a round of drink was called for, and the publican answered the call. Some of the company had whisky to drink, and others had porter or ale, whichever they liked best; as for myself, I remember I had gingerbeer. Well, when we had all partaken of a little drink, it was proposed by some one in the company that a chairman should be elected for the evening, which seemed to meet with the publican's approbation. Then the chairman was elected, and I was introduced to the company by the chairman as the great poet M'Gonagall, who was going to give them an entertainment from his own productions; hoping they would keep good order and give me a fair hearing, and, if they would, he was sure I would please them. And when he had delivered himself so, he told me to begin, and accordingly I did so, and entertained the company for about an hour and a half. The company was highly satisfied with the entertainment I gave them, and everyone in the company gave threepence each, or sixpence each — whatever they liked, I suppose — until it amounted to five shillings. Then the chairman told the publican that five shillings had been subscribed anent the entertainment I had given, and handed it to him. Then the publican gave it to me, and I thanked him and the company for the money I received from them anent the entertainment I had given them. Then the chairman proposed that I should sing "The Rattling Boy from Dublin" over again, and that would conclude the evening's entertainment, and that I would get another subscription, which was unanimously carried by the company, but opposed by the publican; and he told me and the company I had no right to get any more than I had bargained for. But, my friends, his motive for objecting to me getting any more money was to get it himself anent another round of drink he guessed the party would have after I left. And such was the case, as I was told by one of the party the next day, who stayed well up to eleven o'clock, and it was after ten o'clock when I left. Now, my friends, here was a man, a publican, I may say, that pretended to be my friend, that was not satisfied with the money that he got from the company for so many rounds of drink, all through me, of course, that had brought them there to hear me give an entertainment. My opinion is, if I had been as simple to have spent my five shillings that I got for giving my entertainment, he would not have felt satisfied either. In my opinion, he would have laughed at my simplicity for doing so. May heaven protect me from all such friends for ever, and protect everyone that reads my experiences amongst the publicans in this little Book of Poetic Gems!

I remember another night while giving an entertainment in a certain public-house to my admirers, and as soon as the publican found out I was getting money for giving the entertainment, he immediately wrote a letter and addressed it to me, or caused some one else to do it for him, and one of the waiters gave it to me. As soon as I received it in my hand I gave it to one of the company to read, and before he broke open the letter I told him it was a hoax, in my opinion, got up to make me leave his house; and, my dear friends, it was just as I thought — a hoax. I was told in that letter, by particular request, to go to Gray's Hall, where a ball was held that evening, and, at the request of the master of the ceremonies, I was requested to come along to the hall, and recite my famous poem, "Bruce of Bannockburn" and I would be remunerated for it, and to hire a cab immediately, for the company at the ball were all very anxious to hear me. So I left the public-house directly, but I was not so foolish as to hire a cab to take me to Gray's Hall. No, my friends, I walked all the way, and called at the hall and shewed the letter to a man that was watching the hall door, and requested him to read it, and to show it to the master of the ball ceremonies, to see if I was wanted to recite my poem, "Bruce of Bannockburn." So the man took the letter from me and shewed it to the master of the ceremonies, and he soon returned with the letter, telling me it was a hoax, which I expected. My dear friends, this lets you see so far, as well as me, that these publicans that won't permit singing or reciting in their houses are the ones that are selfish or cunning. They know right well that while anyone is singing a song in the company, or reciting, it arrests the attention of the audience from off the drink. That is the reason, my dear friends for the publican not allowing moral entertainments to be carried on in their houses, which I wish to impress on your minds. It is not for the sake of making a noise in their houses, as many of them say by way of an excuse. No! believe me, they know that pleasing entertainment arrests the attention of their customers from off the drink for the time being, and that is the chief reason for them not permitting it, and, from my own experience, I know it to be the case. I remember another night while in a public-house. This was on a Saturday night, and the room I was in was quite full, both of men and women, and, of course, I was well known to the most of them. However, I was requested to sing them a song, or give them a recitation, which, of course, I consented to do on one condition, that I was paid for it, which the company agreed to do. So accordingly I sang "The Rattling Boy from Dublin," which was well received by the company. Then they proposed I should recite my Bannockburn poem, which I did, and after I had finished, and partaken of a little refreshment, the company made up for me a

15

handsome collection. Then I began to think it was time for me to leave, as they seemed rather inclined to sing and enjoy themselves. However, when I got up to leave the company, I missed my stick. Lo and behold! it was gone from the place I had left it, and was nowhere to be seen by me or anyone else in the company. And while I was searching for it, and making a great fuss about it, one of the waiters chanced to come in with drink to the company, and he told me it had been taken away; for what purpose, my friends, if you know not, I will tell you: to make me leave the house, because I was getting too much money from the company, and the landlady guessed I would leave the house when I missed my stick, which was really the case.

I remember another Saturday night I was in the same public-house. and I was entertaining a number of gentlemen, and had received a second collection of money from them, and as soon as the landlady found out I was getting so much money, she rushed into the room and ordered me out at once, telling me to "hook it" out of here, and laid hold of me by the arm and showed me to the door.

Another case, I remember, happened to me in Perth; worse, in my opinion, than that. Well, my friends, I chanced to be travelling at the time, and, being in very poor circumstances, I thought I would call at a public-house where I was a little acquainted with the landlord, and ask him if he would allow me to give an entertainment in one of his rooms, and I would feel obliged to him if he would be so kind. Well, however, he consented with a little flattery. Sometimes flattery does well; and in reference to flattery I will quote the beautiful lines of John Dryden the poet: —

"Flattery, like ice, our footing does betray,
Who can tread sure on the smooth slippery way?
Pleased with the fancy, we glide swiftly on,
And see the dangers which we cannot shun."

The entertainment was to come off that night, and to commence at eight o'clock. So, my friends, I travelled around the city — God knows, tired, hungry, and footsore — inviting the people to come and hear me give my entertainment; and, of course, a great number of rich men and poor men came to hear me, and the room was filled by seven o'clock. But, remember, my dear friends, when I wanted to begin, the publican would not allow me until he had almost extracted every penny from the pockets of the company. And when he told me to begin, I remember I felt very reluctant to do so, for I knew I would get but a small recompense for my entertainment. And it just turned out to be as I expected. My dear friends, I only received eighteen-pence for my entertainment from, I daresay, about sixty of a company. I ask of you, my dear readers, how much did the publican realise from the company that night by selling drink? In my opinion, the least he would have realised would be eighteen shillings or a pound. But, depend upon it, they will never take the advantage of me again.

My dear friends, I entreat of you all, for God's sake and for the furtherance of Christ's kingdom, to abstain from all kinds of intoxicating liquor, because seldom any good emanates from it. In the first place, if it was abolished, there would not be so much housebreaking, for this reason: When the burglar wants to break into a house, if he thinks he hasn't got enough courage to do so, he knows that if he takes a few glasses of either rum, whisky, or brandy, it will give him the courage to rob and kill honest disposed people. Yet the Government tolerates such a demon, I may call it, to be sold in society; to help burglars and theives to rob and kill; also to help the seducer to seduce our daughters; and to help to fill our prisons, and our lunatic asylums, and our poorhouses. Therefore, for these few sufficient reasons, I call upon you, fathers and mothers, and the friends of Christianity, and the friends of humanity,

> To join each one, with heart and hand,
> And help to banish the bane of society from our
>   land,
> And trust in God, and worship Him,
> And denounce the publicans, because they cause
>   sin;
> Therefore cease from strong drink,
> And you will likely do well,
> Then there's not so much danger of going to
>   hell!

My dear friends, along with my experiences amongst the publicans, I will relate to you a rather dangerous adventure that happened to me some years ago, as follows. Being on travel in the parish of Liff, that is, I think, about six miles from Dundee, and as I was very hard up for money at the time, and being rather at a loss how to get a little of that filthy lucre, as some people term it. But, my dear readers, I never considered it to be either filthy or bad. Money is most certainly the most useful commodity in society that I know of. It is certainly good when not abused; but, if abused, the fault rests with the abuser — the money is good nevertheless. For my own part, I have always found it to be one of my best friends. Well, being near to a smithy at the time I refer to, I resolved to call on the smith at the smithy and ask his permission to be allowed to give an entertainment from my own works in the smithy that same night. And when I called on the smith and asked his permission to give my entertainment, and told him who I was, he granted me permission of the smithy cheerfully to give my entertainment. So I went from house to house in the district, inviting the people to come to my entertainment, which was to commence at eight o'clock. Admission — adults, twopence each; children, one penny each. When it drew near to eight o'clock there was a very respectable audience gathered to hear me, and gave me a very hearty welcome and a patient hearing; and they all felt highly delighted with the entertainment I had given them, and many of them inviting me to hurry back again, and give them another entertainment. The proceeds, I remember, for the entertainment I gave amounted to four shillings and ninepence, which I was very thankful for. Well, my dear friends, after I had thanked the smith for the liberty of his smithy, and had left and had drawn near to Liff school-room. I heard the pattering of men's feet behind me, and an undefinable fear seized me. Having my umbrella with me I grasped it firmly, and waited patiently until three men came up to me near Liff school-room, and there they stood glaring at me as the serpent does before it leaps upon its prey. Then the man in the centre of the three whispered to his companions, and, as he did so, he threw out both his hands, with the intention, no doubt, of knocking me down, and, with the assistance of the other two, robbing me of the money I had realised from my entertainment. But when he threw out his arms to catch hold of me, as quick as lightning I struck him a blow across the legs with my umbrella, which made him leap backwards, and immediately they then went away round to the front of the school-master's house, close by the road side, and planted themselves there. And when I saw they were waiting for me to come that way as they expected, I resolved to make my escape from them the best way I could. But how? ah, that was the rub. However, I went round to the front of the school-master's house, and reviewed them in the distance, and, the night being dark, the idea struck me if I could manage to get away from their sight they would give up the chase, and go home to Lochee without satisfying their evil intentions. Well, my friends, the plan I adopted was by lowering my body slowly downwards until my knees were touching the ground, and, in that position, I remained for a few seconds; then I threw myself flat on my face on the road, and I remained in that way watching them in the greatest fear imaginable. But, thank God the plan I adopted had the desired effect of saving me from being robbed, or perhaps murdered. Then I thought it advisable to go home by Birkhill, for fear of meeting the night poachers or prowlers again. And when I arrived at Birkhill I resolved to go home by passing through Lord Duncan's woods. I considered it would be safer doing so than by going home the way the poachers had gone, and, just as I made my entry into Lord Duncan's woods, I began to sing—

Yea, though I walk in death's dark vale,
    Yet will I fear none ill,

> For Thou art with me, and Thy rod
>   And staff me comfort still.

So, my dear readers, I arrived safe home, and thanked God for delivering me from the hands of evil-doers, as He has done on all occasions.

Faithfully Yours
William McGonagall
poet, and Tragedian.

ODE TO THE QUEEN
ON HER JUBILEE YEAR

SOUND drums and trumpets, far and near!
And let all Queen Victoria's subjects loudly cheer!
And show by their actions that her they revere,
Because she's served them faithfully fifty long year!

All hail to the Empress of India and Great Britain's Queen!
Long may she live happy and serene!
And as this is now her Jubilee year,
I hope her subjects will show their loyalty without fear.

Therefore let all her subjects rejoice and sing,
Until they make the welkin ring;
And let young and old on this her Jubilee be glad,
And cry, "Long Live our Queen!" and don't be sad.

She has been a good Queen, which no one dare gainsay,
And I hope God will protect her for many a day;
May He enable her a few more years to reign,
And let all her lieges say — Amen!

Let all hatred towards her be thrown aside
All o'er her dominions broad and wide;
And let all her subjects bear in mind,
By God kings and queens are put in trust o'er mankind.

Therefore rejoice and be glad on her Jubilee day,
And try and make the heart of our Queen feel gay;
Oh! try and make her happy in country and town,
And not with Shakspeare say, "uneasy lies the head that
   wears a crown."

And as this is her first Jubilee year,
And will be her last, I rather fear;
Therefore, sound drums and trumpets cheerfully,
Until the echoes are heard o'er land and sea.

And let the innocent voices of the children at home or abroad
Ascend with cheerful shouts to the throne of God;
And sing aloud, "God Save our Gracious Queen!"
Because a good and charitable Sovereign she has been.

Therefore, ye sons of Great Britain, come join with me,
And welcome in our noble Queen's Jubilee;
Because she has been a faithful Queen, ye must confess,
There hasn't been her equal since the days of Queen Bess

Therefore let all her lieges shout and cheer,
"God Save our Gracious Queen!" for many a year;
Let such be the cry in the peasant's cot, and hall,
With stentorian voices, as loud as they can bawl.

And let bonfires be kindled on every hill,
And her subjects dance around them at their freewill;
And try to drive dull care away
By singing and rejoicing on the Queen's Jubilee day.

May God protect her for many a day,
At home or abroad when she's far away;
Long may she be spared o'er her subjects to reign,
And let each and all with one voice say — Amen!

Victoria is a good Queen, which all her subjects know,
And for that may God protect her from every foe;
May He be as a hedge around her, as He's been all along,
And let her live and die in peace — is the end of my song.

26

DEATH OF LORD AND LADY DALHOUSIE

Alas! Lord and Lady Dalhousie are dead, and buried at last,
Which causes many people to feel a little downcast;
And both lie side by side in one grave,
But I hope God in His goodness their souls will save.

And may He protect their children that are left behind,
And may they always food and raiment find;
And from the paths of virtue may they ne'er be led,
And may they always find a house wherein to lay their head.

Lord Dalhousie was a man worthy of all praise,
And to his memory I hope a monument the people will raise,
That will stand for many ages to come
To commemorate the good deeds he has done.

He was beloved by men of high and low degree,
Especially in Forfarshire by his tenantry:
And by many of the inhabitants in and around Dundee.
Because he was affable in temper, and void of all vanity.

He had great affection for his children, also his wife,
'Tis said he loved her as dear as his life;
And I trust they are now in heaven above,
Where all is joy, peace, and love.

At the age of fourteen he resolved to go to sea,
So he entered the training-ship Britannia belong the
    navy,
And entered as a midshipman as he considered most fit,
Then passed through the course of training with the greatest
    credit.

In a short time he obtained the rank of lieutenant,
Then to her Majesty's ship Galatea he was sent;
Which was under the command of the Duke of Edinburg,
And during his service there he felt but little sorrow.

And from that he was promoted to be commander of the
    Britannia,
And was well liked by the men, for what he said was law;
And by him Prince Albert Victor and Prince George received
    a naval education,
Which met with the Prince of Wales' most hearty approbation

'Twas in the year 1877 he married the Lady Ada Louisa
    Bennett,
And by marrying that noble lady he ne'er did regret;
And he was ever ready to give his service in any way,
Most willingly and cheerfully by night or by day.

'Twas in the year of 1887, and on Thursday the 1st of
    December,
Which his relatives and friends will long remember
That were present at the funeral in Cockpen churchyard,
Because they had for the noble Lord a great regard.

About eleven o'clock the remains reached Dalhousie,
And were met by a body of the tenantry;
They conveyed them inside the building, all seemingly woe
    begone,
And among those that sent wreaths was Lord Claude
    Hamilton.

Those that sent wreaths were but very few,
But one in particular was the Duke of Bucceleuch;
Besides Dr Herbert Spencer, and Countess Rosebery, and
    Lady Bennett,
Which no doubt were sent by them with heartfelt regret.

Besides those that sent wreaths in addition were the Earl
    and Countess of Aberdeen,
Especially the Prince of Wales' was most lovely to be seen,
And the Earl of Dalkeith's wreath was very pretty too,
With a mixture of green and white flowers, beautiful to
    view.

Amongst those present at the interment were Mr Marjoribanks.
    M.P.,
Also ex-Provost Ballingall from Bonnie Dundee;
Besides the Honourable W. G. Colville, representing the
    Duke and Duchess of Edinburgh,
While in every one's face standing at the grave was depicted
    sorrow.

The funeral service was conducted in the Church of Cockpen
By the Rev. J. Crabb, of St. Andrew's Episcopal Church,
    town of Brechin;
And as the two coffins were lowered into their last resting.
    place,
Then the people retired with sad hearts at a quick pace.

DEATH OF PRINCE LEOPOLD

ALAS! noble Prince Leopold, he is dead!
Who often has his lustre shed:
Especially by singing for the benefit of Esher School,—
Which proves he was a wise prince, and no conceited fool.

Methinks I see him on the platform singing the *Sands o' Dee*,
The generous-hearted Leopold, the good and the free,
Who was manly in his actions, and beloved by his mother;
And in all the family she hasn't got such another.

He was of a delicate constitution all his life,
And he was his mother's favourite, and very kind to his wife,
And he had also a particular liking for his child,
And in his behaviour he was very mild.

Oh! noble-hearted Leopold, most beautiful to see,
Who was wont to fill your audience's hearts with glee,
With your charming songs, and lectures against strong drink:
Britain had nothing else to fear, as far as you could think.

A wise prince you were, and well worthy of the name,
And to write in praise of thee I cannot refrain;
Because you were ever ready to defend that which is right,
Both pleasing and righteous in God's eye-sight.

And for the loss of such a prince the people will mourn,
But, alas! unto them he can never more return,
Because sorrow never could revive the dead again,
Therefore to weep for him is all in vain.

'Twas on Saturday the 12th of April, in the year 1884,
He was buried in the royal vault, never to rise more
Until the great and fearful judgment-day,
When the last trump shall sound to summon him away.

When the Duchess of Albany arrived she drove through the
    Royal Arch,—
A little before the Seaforth Highlanders set out on the funeral
    march;
And she was received with every sympathetic respect,
Which none of the people present seem'd to neglect.

Then she entered the memorial chapel and stayed a short time,
And as she viewed her husband's remains it was really sublime,
While her tears fell fast on the coffin lid without delay,
Then she took one last fond look, and hurried away.

At half-past ten o'clock the Seaforth Highlanders did appear,
And every man in the detachment his medals did wear;
And they carried their side-arms by their side,
With mournful looks, but full of love and pride.

Then came the Coldstream Guards headed by their band,
Which made the scene appear imposing and grand;
Then the musicians drew up in front of the guard-room,
And waited patiently to see the prince laid in the royal tomb.

First in the procession were the servants of His late Royal
    Highness,
And next came the servants of the Queen in deep mourning
    dress,
And the gentlemen of his household in deep distress,
Also General Du Pla, who accompanied the remains from
    Cannes.

The coffin was borne by eight Highlanders of his own regiment,
And the fellows seemed to be rather discontent
For the loss of the prince they loved most dear,
While adown their cheeks stole many a silent tear.

Then behind the corpse came the Prince of Wales in field
    marshal uniform,
Looking very pale, dejected, careworn, and forlorn;
Then followed great magnates, all dressed in uniform,
And last, but not least, the noble Marquis of Lorne.

The scene in George's Chapel was most magnificent to behold,
The banners of the knights of the garter embroidered with gold;
Then again it was most touching and lovely to see
The Seaforth Highlanders' inscription to the Prince's memory:

It was wrought in violets, upon a background of white flowers,
And as they gazed upon it their tears fell in showers;
But the whole assembly were hushed when Her Majesty did
    appear,
Attired in her deepest mourning, and from her eye there fell
    a tear.

Her Majesty was unable to stand long, she was overcome
    with grief,
And when the Highlanders lowered the coffin into the tomb
    she felt relief;
Then the ceremony closed with singing "Lead, kindly light,"
Then the Queen withdrew in haste from the mournful sight.

Then the Seaforth Highlanders' band played "Lochaber no
    more,"
While the brave soldiers' hearts felt depressed and sore;
And as homeward they marched they let fall many a tear
For the loss of the virtuous Prince Leopold they loved so dear

FUNERAL OF THE GERMAN EMPEROR

Ye sons of Germany, your noble Emperor William now is
dead,
Who oft great armies to battle hath led;
He was a man beloved by his subjects all,
Because he never tried them to enthral.

The people of Germany have cause now to mourn
The loss of their hero, who to them will ne'er return;
But his soul I hope to Heaven has fled away,
To the realms of endless bliss for ever and aye.

He was much respected throughout Europe by the high and
the low,
And all over Germany people's hearts are full of woe;
For in the battlefield he was a hero bold,
Nevertheless, a lover of peace, to his credit be it told.

'Twas in the year of 1888, and an March the 16th day,
That the peaceful William's remains were conveyed away
To the royal mausoleum of Charlottenburg, their last resting
place,
The God-fearing man that never did his country disgrace.

The funeral service was conducted in the cathedral by the
court chaplain, Dr Kogel,
Which touched the hearts of his hearers, as from his lips it
fell,
And in conclusion he recited the Lord's Prayer
In the presence of kings, princes, dukes, and counts assembled
there.

And at the end of the service the infantry outside fired
    volley after volley,
While the people inside the cathedral felt melancholy,
As the sound of the musketry smote upon the ear,
In honour of the illustrious William, whom they loved most dear,

Then there was a solemn pause as the kings and princes
    took their places,
Whilst the hot tears are trickling down their faces,
And the mourners from shedding tears couldn't refrain;
And in respect of the good man, above the gateway glared a
    bituminous flame.

Then the coffin was placed on the funeral car,
By the kings and princes that came from afar;
And the Crown Prince William heads the procession alone,
While behind him are the four heirs-apparent to the throne.

Then followed the three Kings of Saxony, and the King of
    the Belgians also,
Together with the Prince of Wales, with their hearts full of woe,
Besides the Prince of Naples and Prince Rudolph óf Austria
    were there,
Also the Czarevitch, and other princes in their order I do
    declare.

And as the procession passes the palace the blinds are drawn
    completely,
And every house is half hidden with the sable drapery;
And along the line of march expansive arches were erected,
While the spectators standing by seemed very dejected.

And through the Central Avenue, to make the decorations
    complete,
There were pedestals erected, rising fourteen to fifteen feet,

And at the foot and top of each pedestal were hung decorations
    of green bay,
Also beautiful wreaths and evergreen festoons all in grand
    array.

And there were torches fastened on pieces of wood stuck in
    the ground;
And as the people gazed on the wierd-like scene, their silence
    was profound;
And the shopkeepers closed their shops, and hotel-keepers
    closed in the doorways,
And with torchlight and gaslight, Berlin for once was all ablaze.

The authorities of Berlin in honour of the Emperor considered
    it no sin,
To decorate with crape the beautiful city of Berlin;
Therefore Berlin I declare was a city of crape,
Because few buildings crape decoration did escape.

First in the procession was the Emperor's bobyguard,
And his great love for them nothing could it retard;
Then followed a squadron of the hussars with their band,
Playing "Jesus, Thou my Comfort," most solemn and grand.

And to see the procession passing the sightseers tried their best,
Especially when the cavalry hove in sight, riding four abreast;
Men and officers with their swords drawn, a magnificent sight
    to see
In the dim sun's rays, their burnished swords glinting dimly.

Then followed the footguards with slow and solemn tread,
Playing the "Dead March in Saul," most appropriate for the
    dead;
And behind them followed the artillery, with four guns
    abreast,
Also the ministers and court offcials dressed in their best.

The whole distance to the grave was covered over with laurel
    and bay,
So that the body should be borne along smoothly all the way;
And the thousands of banners in the procession were beautiful
    to view,
Because they were composed of cream-coloured silk and light
    blue.

There were thousands of thousands of men and women
    gathered there,
And standing ankle deep in snow, and seemingly didn't care
So as they got a glimpse of the funeral car,
Especially the poor souls that came from afar.

And when the funeral car appeared there was a general hush,
And the spectators in their anxiety to see began to crush;
And when they saw the funeral car by the Emperor's charger
    led,
Every hat and cap was lifted reverently from off each head.

And as the procession moved on the royal mausoleum,
The spectators remained bareheaded and seemingly quite
    dumb;
And as the coffin was borne into its last resting-place,
Sorrow seemed depicted in each one's face.

And after the burial service the mourners took a last farewell
Of the noble-heated William they loved so well;
Then rich and poor dispersed quietly that were assembled
    there,
While two batteries of field-guns fired a sa ute which did
    rend the air
In honour of the immortal hero they loved so dear,
The founder of the Fatherland Germany, that he did revere.

THE FAMOUS TAY WHALE

'Twas in the month of December, and in the year 1883,
That a monster whale came to Dundee,
Resolved for a few days to sport and play,
And devour the small fishes in the silvery Tay.

So the monster whale did sport and play
Among the innocent little fishes in the beautiful Tay,
Until he was seen by some men one day,
And they resolved to catch him without delay.

When it came to be known a whale was seen in the Tay,
Some men began to talk and to say,
We must try and catch this monster of a whale,
So come on, brave boys, and never say fail.

Then the people together in crowds did run,
Resolved to capture the whale and to have some fun!
So small boats were launched on the silvery Tay,
While the monster of the deep did sport and play.

Oh! it was a most fearful and beautiful sight,
To see it lashing the water with its tail all its might,
And making the water ascend like a shower of hail,
With one lash of its ugly and mighty tail.

Then the water did descend on the men in the boats,
Which wet their trousers and also their coats;
But it only made them the more determined to catch the whale,
But the whale shook at them his tail.

Then the whale began to puff and to blow,
While the men and the boats after him did go,
Armed well with harpoons for the fray,
Which they fired at him without dismay.

And they laughed and grinned just like wild baboons,
While they fired at him their sharp harpoons:
But when struck with the harpoons he dived below,
Which filled his pursuers' hearts with woe:

Because they guessed they had lost a prize,
Which caused the tears to well up in their eyes;
And in that their anticipations were only right,
Because he sped on to Stonehaven with all his might:

And was first seen by the crew of a Gourdon fishing boat,
Which they thought was a big coble upturned afloat;
But when they drew near they saw it was a whale,
So they resolved to tow it ashore without fail.

So they got a rope from each boat tied round his tail,
And landed their burden at Stonehaven without fail;
And when the people saw it their voices they did raise,
Declaring that the brave fishermen deserved great praise.

And my opinion is that God sent the whale in time of need,
No matter what other people may think or what is their creed;
I know fishermen in general are often very poor,
And God in His goodness sent it to drive poverty from their
    door.

So Mr John Wood has bought it for two hundred and twenty-six
    pound,
And has brought it to Dundee all safe and all sound;
Which measures 40 feet in length from the snout to the tail,
So I advise the people far and near to see it without fail.

Then hurrah! for the mighty monster whale,
Which has got 17 feet 4 inches from tip to tip of a tail!
Which can be seen for a sixpence or a shilling,
That is to say, if the people all are willing.

THE BATTLE OF TEL-EL-KEBIR

Ye sons of Great Britain, come join with me,
And sing in praise of Sir Garnet Wolseley;
Sound drums and trumpets cheerfully,
For he has acted most heroically.

Therefore loudly his praises sing
Until the hills their echoes back doth ring;
For he is a noble hero bold,
And an honour to his Queen and country, be it told.

He has gained for himself fame and renown,
Which to posterity will be handed down;
Because he has defeated Arabi by land and by sea,
And from the battle of Tel-el-Kebir he made him to flee.

With an army about fourteen thousand strong,
Through Egypt he did fearlessly march along,
With the gallant and brave Highland brigade,
To whom honour is due, be it said.

Arabi's army was about seventy thousand in all,
And, virtually speaking, it wasn't very small;
But if they had been as numerous again,
The Irish and Highland brigades would have beaten them, it
    is plain.

'Twas on the 13th day of September, in the year of 1882,
Which Arabi and his rebel horde long will rue;
Because Sir Garnet Wolseley and his brave little band
Fought and conquered them on Kebir land.

He marched upon the enemy with his gallant band
O'er the wild and lonely desert sand,
And attacked them before daylight,
And in twenty minutes he put them to flight.

The first shock of the attack was borne by the Second Brigade,
Who behaved most manfully, it is said,
Under the command of brave General Grahame,
And have gained a lasting honour to their name.

But Major Hart and the 18th Royal Irish, conjoint,
Carried the trenches at the bayonet's point;
Then the Marines chased them about four miles away,
At the charge of the bayonet, without dismay!

General Sir Archibald Alison led on the Highland Brigade,
Who never were the least afraid.
And such has been the case in this Egyptian war,
For at the charge of the bayonet they ran from them afar!

With their bagpipes playing, and one ringing cheer,
And the 42nd soon did the trenches clear;
Then hand to hand they did engage,
And fought like tigers in a cage.

Oh! it must have been a glorious sight
To see Sir Garnet Wolseley in the thickest of the fight!
In the midst of shot and shell, and the cannon's roar,
Whilst the dead and the dying lay weltering in their gore.

Then the Egyptians were forced to yield,
And the British were left masters of the field;
Then Arabi he did fret and frown
To see his army thus cut down.

Then Arabi the rebel took to flight,
And spurred his Arab steed with all his might:
With his heart full of despair and woe,
And never halted till he reached Cairo.

Now since the Egyptian war is at an end,
let us thank God! Who did send
Sir Garnet Wolseley to crush and kill
Arabi and his rebel army at Kebir hill.

THE RAILWAY BRIDGE OF THE SILVERY TAY

Beautiful Railway Bridge of the Silvery Tay!
With your numerous arches and pillars in so grand array,
And your central girders, which seem to the eye
To be almost towering to the sky.
The greatest wonder of the day,
And a great beautification to the River Tay,
Most beautiful to be seen,
Near by Dundee and the Magdalen Green.

Beautiful Railway Bridge of the Silvery Tay!
That has caused the Emperor of Brazil to leave
His home far away, *incognito* in his dress,
And view thee ere he passed along *en route* to Inverness.

Beautiful Railway Bridge of the Silvery Tay!
The longest of the present day
That has ever crossed o'er a tidal river stream,
Most gigantic to be seen,
Near by Dundee and the Magdalen Green.

Beautiful Railway Bridge of the Silvery Tay!
Which will cause great rejoicing on the opening day,
And hundreds of people will come from far away,
Also the Queen, most gorgeous to be seen,
Near by Dundee and the Magdalen Green.

Beautiful Railway Bridge of the Silvery Tay!
And prosperity to Provost Cox, who has given
Thirty thousand pounds and upwards away
In helping to erect the Bridge of the Tay,
Most handsome to be seen,
Near by Dundee and the Magdalen Green.

Beautiful Railway Bridge of the Silvery Tay!
I hope that God will protect all passengers
By night and by day,
And that no accident will befall them while crossing
The Bridge of the Silvery Tay,
For that would be most awful to be seen
Near by Dundee and the Magdalen Green.

Beautiful Railway Bridge of the Silvery Tay!
And prosperity to Messrs Bouche and Grothe,
The famous engineers of the present day,
Who have succeeded in erecting the Railway
Bridge of the Silvery Tay,
Which stands unequalled to be seen
Near by Dundee and the Magdalen Green.

THE NEWPORT RAILWAY

Success to the Newport Railway,
Along the braes of the Silvery Tay,
And to Dundee straightway,
Across the Railway Bridge o' the Silvery Tay,
Which was opened on the 12th of May,
In the year of our Lord 1879,
Which will clear all expenses in a very short time
Because the thrifty housewives of Newport
To Dundee will often resort,
Which will be to them profit and sport,
By bringing cheap tea, bread, and jam,
And also some of Lipton's ham,
Which will make their hearts feel light and gay,
And cause them to bless the opening day
Of the Newport Railway.

The train is most beautiful to be seen,
With its long, white curling cloud of steam,
As the train passes on her way
Along the bonnie braes o' the Silvery Tay.

And if the people of Dundee
Should feel inclined to have a spree,
I am sure 'twill fill their hearts with glee
By crossing o'er to Newport,
And there they can have excellent sport,
By viewing the scenery beautiful and gay,
During the livelong summer day.

And then they can return at night
With spirits light and gay,
By the Newport Railway,
By night or by day,
Across the Railway Bridge o' the Silvery Tay.

Success to the undertakers of the Newport Railway
Hoping the Lord will their labours repay,
And prove a blessing to the people
For many a long day
Who live near by Newport,
On the bonnie braes o' the Silvery Tay.

ADDRESS TO THE NEW TAY BRIDGE

Beautiful new railway bridge of the Silvery Tay,
With your strong brick piers and buttresses in so grand array.
And your thirteen central girders, which sem to my eye
Strong enough all windy storms to defy.
And as I gaze upon thee my heart feels gay,
Because thou are the greatest railway bridge of the present day,
And can be seen for miles away
From north, south, east, or west of the Tay
On a beautiful and clear sunshiny day,
And ought to make the hearts of the "Mars" boys feel gay,
Because thine equal nowhere can be seen,
Only near by Dundee and the bonnie Magdalen Green.

Beautiful new railway bridge of the Silvery Tay,
With thy beautiful side-screens along your railway,
Which will be a great protection on a windy day,
So as the railway carriages won't be blown away,
And ought to cheer the hearts of the passengers night and day
As they are conveyed along thy beautiful railway,
And towering above the silvery Tay,
Spanning the beautiful river shore to shore
Upwards of two miles and more,
Which is most wonderful to be seen
Near by Dundee and the bonnie Magdalen Green.

Thy structure to my eye seems strong and grand,
And the workmanship most skilfully planned;
And I hope the designers, Messrs Barlow & Arrol, will prosper
    for many a day
For erecting thee across the beautiful Tay.
And I think nobody need have the least dismay
To cross o'er thee by night or by day,
Because thy strength is visible to be seen
Near by Dundee and the bonnie Magdalen Green.

Beautiful new railway bridge of the Silvery Tay
I wish you success for many a year and a day,
And I hope thousands of people will come from far away,
Both high and low without delay,
From the north, south, east, and the west,
Because as a railway bridge thou are the best;
Thou standest unequalled to be seen
Near by Dundee and the bonnie Magdalen Green.

And for beauty thou art most lovely to be seen
As the train crosses o'er thee with her cloud of steam;
And you look well, painted the colour of marone,
And to find thy equal there is none,
Which, without fear of contradiction, I venture to say,
Because you are the longest railway bridge of the present day
That now crosses o'er a tidal river stream,
And the most handsome to be seen
Near by Dundee and the bonnie Magdalen Green.

The New Yorkers boast about their Brooklyn Bridge,
But in comparison to thee it seems like a midge,
Because thou spannest the silvery Tay
A mile and more longer I venture to say;
Besides the railway carriages are pulled across by a rope,
Therefore Brooklyn Bridge cannot with thee cope;
And as you have been opened on the 20th day of June,
I hope Her Majesty Queen Victoria will visit thee very soon,
Because thou are worthy of a visit from Duke, Lord, or Queen,
And strong and securely built, which is most worthy to be seen
Near by Dundee and the bonnie Magdalen Green

THE TAY BRIDGE DISASTER

Beautiful Railway Bridge of the Silv'ry Tay!
Alas! I am very sorry to say
That ninety lives have been taken away
On the last Sabbath day of 1879,
Which will be remember'd for a very long time.

'Twas about seven o'clock at night,
And the wind it blew with all its might,
And the rain came pouring down,
And the dark clouds seem'd to frown,
And the Demon of the air seem'd to say —
"I'll blow down the Bridge of Tay."

When the train left Edinburgh
The passengers' hearts were light and felt no sorrow,
But Boreas blew a terrific gale,
Which made their hearts for to quail,
And many of the passengers with fear did say —
"I hope God will send us safe across the Bridge of Tay."

But when the train came near to Wormit Bay,
Boreas he did loud and angry bray,
And shook the central girders of the Bridge of Tay
On the last Sabbath day of 1879,
Which will be remember'd for a very long time.

So the train sped on with all its might,
And Bonnie Dundee soon hove in sight,
And the passengers' hearts felt light,
Thinking they would enjoy themselves on the New Year,
With their friends at home they lov'd most dear,
And wish them all a happy New Year.

So the train mov'd slowly along the Bridge of Tay,
Until it was about midway,
Then the central girders with a crash gave way,
And down went the train and passengers into the Tay!
The Storm Fiend did loudly bray,
Because ninety lives had been taken away,
On the last Sabbath day of 1879,
Which will be remember'd for a very long time.

As soon as the catastrophe came to be known
The alarm from mouth to mouth was blown,
And the cry rang out all o'er the town,
Good Heavens! the Tay Bridge is blown down,
And a passenger train from Edinburgh,
Which fill'd all the people's hearts with sorrow,
And made them for to turn pale,
Because none of the passengers were sav'd to tell the tale
How the disaster happen'd on the last Sabbath day of 1879
Which will be remember'd for a very long time.

It must have been an awful sight,
To witness in the dusky moonlight,
While the Storm Fiend did laugh, and angry did bray,
Along the Railway Bridge of the Silv'ry Tay.
Oh! ill-fated Bridge of the Silv'ry Tay,
I must now conclude my lay
By telling the world fearlessly without the least dismay,
That your central girders would not have given way,
At least many sensible men do say,
Had they been supported on each side with buttresses,
At least many sensible men confesses,
For the stronger we our houses do build,
¯he less chance we have of being killed.

THE LATE SIR JOHN OGILVY

Alas! Sir John Ogilvy is dead, aged eighty-seven,
But I hope his soul is now in heaven;
For he was a generous-hearted gentleman I am sure,
And, in particular, very kind unto the poor.

He was a Christian gentleman in every degree,
And, for many years, was an M.P. for Bonnie Dundee,
And, while he was an M.P., he didn't neglect
To advocate the rights of Dundee in every respect.

He was a public benefactor in many ways,
Especially in erecting an asylum for imbecile children to
    spend their days;
Then he handed the institution over as free—
As a free gift and a boon to the people of Dundee.

He was chairman of several of the public boards in Dundee,
And among these were the Asylum Board and the Royal
    Infirmary;
In every respect he was a God-fearing true gentleman,
And to gainsay it there's nobody can.

He lived as a Christian gentleman in his time,
And he now lies buried in the family vault in Strathmartine;
But I hope his soul has gone aloft where all troubles cease,
Amongst the blessed saints where all is joy and peace.

To the people around Baldovan he will be a great loss,
Because he was a kind-hearted man and a Soldier of the Cross.
He had always a kind word for every one he met,
And the loss of such a good man will be felt with deep regret.

Because such men as Sir John Ogilvy are hard to be found,
Especially in Christian charity his large heart did abound,
Therefore a monument should be erected for him most handsome
    to behold,
And his good deeds engraven thereon in letters of gold.

THE RATTLING BOY FROM DUBLIN

I'm a rattling boy from Dublin town,
I courted a girl called Biddy Brown,
Her eyes they were as black as sloes,
She had black hair and an aquiline nose.

Chorus —

Whack fal de da, fal de darelido,
Whack fal de da, fal de darelay,
Whack fal de da, fal de darelido,
Whack fal de da, fal de darelay.

One night I met her with another lad,
Says I, Biddy, I've caught you, by dad;
I never thought you were half so bad
As to be going about with another lad.

Chorus.

Says I, Biddy, this will never do,
For to-night you've prov'd to me untrue.
So do not make a hullaballoo,
For I will bid farewell to you.

Chorus.

Says Barney Magee, She is my lass,
And the man that says no, he is an ass,
So come away, and I'll give you a glass,
Och, sure you can get another lass.

Chorus

Says I, To the devil with your glass,
You have taken from me my darling lass,
And if you look angry, or offer to frown,
With my darling shillelah I'll knock you down

Chorus.

Says Barney Magee unto me,
By the hokey I love Biddy Brown,
And before I'll give her up to thee,
One or both of us will go down.

Chorus.

So, with my darling shillelah, I gave him a whack
Which left him lying on his back,
Saying, botheration to you and Biddy Brown —
For I'm the rattling boy from Dublin town.

Chorus.

So a policeman chanced to come up at the time,
And he asked of me the cause of the shine,
Says, I, he threatened to knock me down
When I challenged him for walking with my Biddy Brown

Chorus.

So the policeman took Barney Magee to jail,
Which made him shout and bewail
That ever he met with Biddy Brown,
The greatest deceiver in Dublin town.

Chorus.

So I bade farewell to Biddy Brown,
The greatest jilter in Dublin town,
Because she proved untrue to me,
And was going about with Barney Magee.

Chorus.

BURIAL OF THE REV. GEORGE GILFILLAN

On the Gilfillan burial day,
In the Hill o' Balgay,
It was a most solemn sight to see,
Not fewer than thirty thousand people assembled in Dundee,
All watching the funeral procession of Gilfillan that day,
That death had suddenly taken away,
And was going to be buried in the Hill o' Balgay.

There were about three thousand people in the procession alone,
And many were shedding tears, and several did moan,
And their bosoms heaved with pain,
Because they knew they would never look upon his like again.

There could not be fewer than fifty carriages in the procession
    that day,
And gentlemen in some of them that had come from far away,
And in whispers some of them did say,
As the hearse bore the precious corpse away,
Along the Nethergate that day.
I'm sure he will be greatly missed by the poor,
For he never turned them empty-handed away from his door;
And to assist them in distress it didn't give him pain,
And I'm sure the poor will never look upon his like again.

On the Gilfillan burial day, in the Hill o' Balgay,
There was a body of policemen marshalled in grand array,
And marched in front of the procession all the way;
Also the relatives and friends of the deceas'd,
Whom I hope from all sorrows has been releas'd,
And whose soul I hope to heaven has fled away,
To sing with saints above for ever and aye.

The Provost, Magistrates, and Town Council were in the
    procession that day;
Also Mrs Gilfillan, who cried and sobbed all the way
For her kind husband, that was always affable and gay,
Which she will remember until her dying day.

When the procession arrived in the Hill o' Balgay,
The people were almost as hush as death, and many of them
    did say —
As long as we live we'll remember the day
That the great Gilfillan was buried in the Hill o' Balgay.

When the body of the great Gilfillan was lowered into the grave,
'Twas then the people's hearts with sorrow did heave;
And with tearful eyes and bated breath,
Mrs Gilfillan lamented her loving husband's death.

Then she dropped a ringlet of immortelles into his grave,
Then took one last fond look, and in sorrow did leave;
And all the people left with sad hearts that day,
And that ended the Gilfillan burial in the Hill o' Balgay.

THE BATTLE OF EL-TEB

Ye sons of Great Britain, I think no shame
To write in praise of brave General Graham!
Whose name will be handed down to posterity without any
    stigma,
Because, at the battle of El-Teb, he defeated Osman Digna.

With an army about five thousand strong,
To El-Teb, in the year 1884, he marched along,
And bivouacked there for the night;
While around their fires they only thought of the coming fight.

They kept up their fires all the long night,
Which made the encampment appear weird-like to the sight;
While the men were completely soaked with the rain,
But the brave heroes disdained to complain.

The brave heroes were glad when daylight did appear,
And when the reveille was sounded, they gave a hearty cheer
And their fires were piled up higher again,
Then they tried to dry their clothes that were soaked with
    the rain.

Then breakfast was taken about eight o'clock,
And when over, each man stood in the ranks as firm as a rock,
And every man seemed to be on his guard—
All silent and ready to move forward.

The first movement was a short one from where they lay—
Then they began to advance towards El-Teb without dismay,
And showed that all was in order for the fray,
While every man's heart seemed to feel light and gay.

The enemy's position could be seen in the distance far away
But the brave heroes marched on without delay—
Whilst the enemy's banners floated in the air,
And dark swarms of men were scattered near by there.

Their force was a large one — its front extended over a mile,
And all along the line their guns were all in file;
But, as the British advanced, they disappeared,
While our brave kilty lads loudly cheered.

Thus slowly and cautiously brave General Graham proceeded,
And to save his men from slaughter, great caution was needed,
Because Osman Digna's force was about ten thousand strong;
But he said, Come on, my brave lads, we'll conquer them
    ere long!

It was about ten o'clock when they came near the enemy's lines,
And on the morning air could be heard the cheerful chimes
Coming from the pipes of the gallant Black Watch,
Which every ear in the British force was eager to catch.

Then they passed by the enemy about mid-day,
While every Arab seemed to have his gun ready for the fray;
When a bullet strikes down General Baker by the way,
But he is soon in the saddle again without delay.

And ready for any service that he could perform;
Whilst the bullets fell around them in a perfect storm
That they had to lie down, but not through fear,
Because the enemy was about 800 yards on their left rear.

Then General Graham addressed his men,
And said, If they won't attack us, we must attack them,
So start to your feet my lads, and never fear,
And strike up your bagpipes, and give a loud cheer.

So they leapt to their feet, and gave a loud cheer,
While the Arabs swept down upon them without the least fear,
And put aside their rifles, and grasped their spears;
Whilst the British bullets in front of them the earth uptears.

Then the British charged them with their cold steel,
Which made the Arabs backward for to reel;

But they dashed forward again on their ranks without dismay,
But before the terrible fire of their musketry they were
    swept away.

Oh, God of Heaven; it was a terrible sight
To see, and hear the Arabs shouting with all their might
A fearful oath when they got an inch of cold steel,
Which forced them backwards again, and made them reel.

By two o'clock they were fairly beat,
And Osman Digna, the false prophet, was forced to retreat
After three hours of an incessant fight;
But Heaven, 'tis said, defends the right.

And I think he ought to be ashamed of himself;
For I consider he has acted the part of a silly elf,
By thinking to conquer the armies of the Lord
With his foolish and benighted rebel horde.

THE BATTLE OF ABU KLEA

Ye sons of Mars, come join with me,
And sing in praise of Sir Herbert Stewart's little army,
That made ten thousand Arabs flee
At the charge of the bayonet at Abu Klea.

General Stewart's force was about fifteen hundred all told,
A brave little band, but, like lions bold,
They fought under their brave and heroic commander,
As gallant and as skilful as the great Alexander.

And the nation has every reason to be proud,
And in praise of his little band we cannot speak too loud,
Because that gallant fifteen hundred soon put to flight
Ten thousand Arabs, which was a most beautiful sight.

The enemy kept up a harmless fire all night,
And threw up works on General Stewart's right;
Therefore he tried to draw the enemy on to attack,
But they hesitated, and through fear drew back.

But General Stewart ordered his men forward in square,
All of them on foot, ready to die and to dare;
And he forced the enemy to engage in the fray,
But in a short time they were glad to run away.

But not before they penetrated through the British square,
Which was a critical moment to the British, I declare,
Owing to the great number of the Arabs,
Who rushed against their bayonets and received fearful stabs.

Then all was quiet again until after breakfast,
And when the brave little band had finished their repast,
Then the firing began from the heights on the right,
From the breastworks they had constructed during the night.

By eight o'clock the enemy was of considerable strength,
With their banners waving beautifully and of great length,
And creeping steadily up the grassy road direct to the wells,
But the British soon checked their advance by shot and shells.

At ten o'clock brave General Stewart made a counter-attack,
Resolved to turn the enemy on a different track;
And he ordered his men to form a hollow square,
Placing the Guards in the front, and telling them to prepare.

And on the left was the Mounted Infantry,
Which truly was a magnificent sight to see;
Then the Sussex Regiment was on the right,
And the Heavy Cavalry and Naval Brigade all ready to fight.

Then General Stewart took up a good position on a slope,
Where he guessed the enemy could not with him cope,
Where he knew the rebels must advance,
All up hill and upon open ground, which was his only chance.

Then Captain Norton's battery planted shells amongst the
    densest mass,
Determined with shot and shell the enemy to harass;
Then came the shock of the rebels against the British square,
While the fiendish shouts of the Arabs did rend the air.

But the steadiness of the Guards, Marines, and Infantry
    prevailed,
And for the loss of their brother officers they sadly bewailed,
Who fell mortally wounded in the bloody fray,
Which they will remember for many a long day.

For ten minutes a desperate struggle raged from left to rear,
While Gunner Smith saved Lieutenant Guthrie's life without
    dread or fear;
When all the other gunners had been borne back,
He took up a handspike, and the Arabs he did whack.

The noble hero hard blows did strike,
As he swung round his head the handspike;
He seemed like a destroying angel in the midst of the fight,
The way be scattered the Arabs left and right.

Oh! it was an exciting and terrible sight,
To see Colonel Burnaby engaged in the fight:
With sword in hand, fighting with might and main,
Until killed by a spear-thrust in the jugular vein.

A braver soldier ne'er fought on a battle-field,
Death or glory was his motto, rather than yield;
A man of noble stature and manly to behold,
And an honour to his country be it told.

It was not long before every Arab in the square was killed,
And with a dense smoke and dust the air was filled;
General Stewart's horse was shot, and he fell to the ground,
In the midst of shot and shell on every side around.

And when the victory was won they gave three British cheers,
While adown their cheeks flowed many tears
For their fallen comrades that lay weltering in their gore;
Then the square was re-formed and the battle was o'er.

A CHRISTMAS CAROL

Welcome, sweet Christmas, blest be the morn
That Christ our Saviour was born!
Earth's Redeemer, to save us from all danger,
And, as the Holy Record tells, born in a manger.

   Chorus — Then ring, ring, Christmas bells,
      Till your sweet music o'er the kingdom swells
      To warn the people to respect the morn
      That Christ their Saviour was born.

The snow was on the ground when Christ was born,
And the Virgin Mary His mother felt very forlorn
As she lay in a horse's stall at a roadside inn,
Till Christ our Saviour was born to free us from sin.

Oh! think of the Virgin Mary as she lay
In a lowly stable on a bed of hay,
And angels watching o'er her till Christ was born,
Therefore all the people should respect Christmas morn.

The way to respect Christmas time
Is not by drinking whisky or wine,
But to sing praises to God on Christmas morn,
The time that Jesus Christ His Son was born;

Whom He sent into the world to save sinners from hell,
And by believing in Him in heaven we'll dwell;
Then blest be the morn that Christ was born,
Who can save us from hell, death, and scorn.

Then be warned, and respect the Saviour dear,
And treat with less respect the New Year,
And respect always the blessed morn
That Christ our Saviour was born.

For each new morn to the Christian is dear,
As well as the morn of the New Year,
And he thanks God for the light of each new morn,
Especially the morn that Christ was born.

Therefore, good people, be warned in time,
And on Christmas morn don't get drunk with wine,
But praise God above on Christmas morn,
Who sent His Son to save us from hell and scorn.

There the heavenly babe He lay
In a stall among a lot of hay,
While the Angel Host by Bethlehem
Sang a beautiful and heavenly anthem.

Christmas time ought to be held most dear,
Much more so than the New Year,
Because that's the time that Christ was born,
Therefore respect Christmas morn.

And let the rich be kind to the poor,
And think of the hardships they do endure,
Who are neither clothed nor fed,
And many without a blanket to their bed

THE CHRISTMAS GOOSE

Mr Smiggs was a gentleman,
 And lived in London town;
His wife she was a good kind soul,
 And seldom known to frown.

'Twas on Christmas eve,
 And Smiggs and his wife lay cosy in bed,
When the thought of buying a goose
 Came into his head.

So the next morning,
 Just as the sun rose,
He jump'd out of bed,
 And he donn'd his clothes,

Saying, "Peggy, my dear,
 You need not frown,
For I'll buy you the best goose
 In all London town."

So away to the poultry shop he goes,
 And bought the goose, as he did propose,
And for it he paid one crown,
 The finest, he thought, in London town.

When Smiggs bought the goose
 He suspected no harm,
But a naughty boy stole it
 From under his arm.

Then Smiggs he cried, "Stop, thief!
 Come back with my goose!"
But the naughty boy laugh'd at him,
 And gave him much abuse.

But a policeman captur'd the naughty boy,
  And gave the goose to Smiggs,
And said he was greatly bother'd
  By a set of juvenile prigs.

So the naughty boy was put in prison
  For stealing the goose,
And got ten days' confinement
  Before he got loose.

So Smiggs ran home to his dear Peggy,
  Saying, "Hurry, and get this fat goose ready,
That I have bought for one crown;
  So, my darling, you need not frown."

"Dear Mr Smiggs, I will not frown:
  I'm sure 'tis cheap for one crown,
Especially at Christmas time—
  Oh! Mr Smiggs, it's really fine."

"Peggy, it is Christmas time,
  So let us drive dull care away,
For we have got a Christmas goose,
  So cook it well, I pray.

"No matter how the poor are clothed,
  Or if they starve at home,
We'll drink our wine, and eat our goose,
  Aye, and pick it to the bone."

AN AUTUMN REVERIE

Alas! beautiful Summer now hath fled,
And the face of Nature doth seem dead,
And the leaves are withered, and falling off the trees,
By the nipping and chilling autumnal breeze.

The pleasures of the little birds are all fled,
And with the cold many of them will be found dead,
Because the leaves of the trees are scattered in the blast,
And makes the feathered creatures feel downcast.

Because there are no leaves on the trees to shield them from
    the storm
On a windy, and rainy, cloudy morn;
Which makes their little hearts throb with pain,
By the chilling blast and the pitiless rain.

But still they are more contented than the children of God,
As long as they can pick up a worm from the sod,
Or anything they can get to eat,
Just, for instance, a stale crust of bread or a grain of wheat.

Oh! think of the little birds in the time of snow,
Also of the little street waifs, that are driven to and fro,
And trembling in the cold blast, and chilled to the bone,
For the want of food and clothing, and a warm home.

Besides think of the sorrows of the wandering poor,
That are wandering in the cold blast from door to door;
And begging, for Heaven's sake, a crust of bread,
And alas! not knowing where to lay their head.

While the rich are well fed and covered from the cold,
While the poor are starving, both young and old;
Alas! it is the case in his boasted Christian land,
Whereas the rich are told to be kind to the poor, is God's
   command.

Oh! think of the working man when he's no work to do,
Who's got a wife and family, perhaps four or two,
And the father searching for work, and no work can be had,
The thought, I'm sure, 'tis enough to drive the poor man mad.

Because for his wife and family he must feel,
And perhaps the thought thereof will cause him to steal
Bread for his family, that are starving at home,
While the thought thereof makes him sigh heavily and groan.

Alas! the pangs of hunger are very hard to thole,
And few people can their temper control,
Or become reconciled to their fate,
Especially when they cannot find anything to eat.

Oh! think of the struggles of the poor to make a living,
Because the rich unto them seldom are giving;
Whereas they are told he that giveth to the poor lendeth
   unto the Lord,
But alas! they rather incline their money to hoard.

Then there's the little news-vendors in the street,
Running about perhaps with bare feet;
And if the rich chance to see such creatures in the street,
In general they make a sudden retreat.

WRECK OF THE STEAMER "LONDON"
WHILE ON HER WAY TO AUSTRALIA

'Twas in the year of 1866, and on a very beautiful day,
That eighty-two passengers, with spirits light and gay,
Left Gravesend harbour, and sailed gaily away
On board the steamship "London,"
Bound for the city of Melbourne,
Which unfortunately was her last run,
Because she was wrecked on the stormy main,
Which has caused many a heart to throb with pain,
Because they will ne'er look upon their lost ones again.

'Twas on the 11th of January they anchored at the Nore;
The weather was charming — the like was seldom seen before
Especially the next morning as they came in sight
Of the charming and beautiful Isle of Wight,
But the wind it blew a terrific gale towards night,
Which caused the passengers' hearts to shake with fright,
And caused many of them to sigh and mourn,
And whisper to themselves, We will ne'er see Melbourne.

Amongst the passengers was Gustavus V. Brooke,
Who was to be seen walking on the poop,
Also clergymen, and bankers, and magistrates also,
All chatting merrily together in the cabin below;
And also wealthy families returning to their dear native land
And accomplished young ladies, most lovely and grand,
All in the beauty and bloom of their pride,
And some with their husbands sitting close by their side.

'Twas all on a sudden the storm did arise,
Which took the captain and passengers all by surprise,
Because they had just sat down to their tea,
When the ship began to roll with the heaving of the sea,
And shipped a deal of water, which came down on their heads,
Which wet their clothes and also their beds;
And caused a fearful scene of consternation,
And amongst the ladies great tribulation,
And made them cry out, Lord, save us from being drowned,
And for a few minutes the silence was profound.

Then the passengers began to run to and fro,
With buckets to bale out the water between decks below,
And Gustavus Brooke quickly leapt from his bed
In his Garibaldi jacket and drawers, without fear or dread,
And rushed to the pump, and wrought with might and main;
But alas! all their struggling was in vain,
For the water fast did on them gain;
But he enacted a tragic part until the last,
And sank exhausted when all succour was past;
While the big billows did lash her o'er,
And the Storm-fiend did laugh and roar.

Oh, Heaven! it must have really been
A most harrowing and pitiful scene
To hear mothers and their children loudly screaming,
And to see the tears adown their pale faces streaming,
And to see a clergyman engaged in prayer,
Imploring God their lives to spare, ...
Whilst the cries of the women and children did rend the air.

Then the captain cried, Lower down the small boats,
And see if either of them sinks or floats;
Then the small boats were launched on the stormy wave,
And each one tried hard his life to save
From a merciless watery grave. . . . . . .

A beautiful young lady did madly cry and rave,
"Five hundred sovereigns, my life to save!"
But she was by the sailors plainly told
For to keep her filthy gold, ...
Because they were afraid to overload the boat,
Therefore she might either sink or float,
Then she cast her eyes to Heaven, and cried, Lord, save me,
Then went down with the ship to the bottom of the sea,
Along with Gustavus Brooke, who was wont to fill our hearts
    with glee
While performing Shakespearian tragedy.

And out of eighty-two passengers only twenty were saved,
And that twenty survivors most heroically behaved.
For three stormy days and stormy nights they were tossed to
    and fro
On the raging billows, with their hearts full of woe,
Alas! poor souls, not knowing where to go,
Until at last they all agreed to steer for the south,
And they chanced to meet an Italian barque bound for
    Falmouth,
And they were all rescued from a watery grave,
And they thanked God and Captain Cavassa, who did their
    lives save.

WRECK OF THE "THOMAS DRYDEN" IN PENTLAND FIRTH

As I stood upon the sandy beach
   One morn near Pentland Ferry,
I saw a beautiful brigantine,
   And all her crew seem'd merry.

When lo! the wind began to howl,
   And the clouds began to frown,
And in the twinkling of an eye
   The rain came pouring down.

Then the sea began to swell,
   And seem'd like mountains high,
And the sailors on board that brigantine
   To God for help did loudly cry.

Oh! it was an awful sight
   To see them struggling with all their might
And imploring God their lives to save
   From a merciless watery grave.

Their cargo consisted of window-glass,
   Also coal and linseed-oil,
Which helped to calm the raging sea
   That loud and angry did boil.

Because when the bottoms of the barrels
   Were with the raging billows stove in,
The oil spread o'er the water,
   And smoothed the stormy billows' din!

Then she began to duck in the trough of the sea
   Which was fearful to behold;
And her crossyards dipped in the big billows
   As from side to side she rolled.

She was tossed about on the merciless sea,
   And received some terrible shocks,
Until at last she ran against
   A jagged reef of rocks.

'Twas then she was rent asunder,
   And the water did rush in —
It was most dreadful to hear it,
   It made such a terrific din.

Then the crew jumped into the small boats
   While the Storm-fiend did roar,
And were very near being drowned
   Before they got ashore.

Then the coal-dust blackened the water
   Around her where she lay,
And the barrels of linseed-oil
   They floated far away.

And when the crew did get ashore,
   They were shaking with cold and fright,
And they went away to Huna inn,
   And got lodgings for the night!

ATTEMPTED ASSASSINATION OF THE QUEEN

God prosper long our noble Queen,
   And long may she reign!
Maclean he tried to shoot her,
   But it was all in vain.

For God He turned the ball aside
   Maclean aimed at her head;
And he felt very angry
   Because he didn't shoot her dead.

There's a divinity that hedgeth a king,
   And so it does seem,
And my opinion is, it has hedged
   Our most gracious Queen.

Maclean must be a madman,
   Which is obvious to be seen,
Or else he wouldn't have tried to shoot
   Our most beloved Queen.

Victoria is a good Queen,
   Which all her subjects know,
And for that God has protected her
   From all her deadly foes.

She is noble and generous,
   Her subjects must confess;
There hasn't been her equal
   Since the days of good Queen Bess.

Long may she be spared to roam
   Among the bonnie Highland floral,
And spend many a happy day
   In the palace of Balmoral.

Because she is very kind
   To the old women there,
And allows them bread, tea, and sugar,
   And each one to get a share.

And when they know of her coming,
   Their hearts feel overjoy'd,
Because, in general, she finds work
   For men that's unemploy'd.

And she also gives the gipsies money
    While at Balmoral, I've been told,
And, mind ye, seldom silver,
    But very often gold.

I hope God will protect her
    By night and by day,
At home and abroad
    When she's far away.

May He be as a hedge around her,
    As He's been all along,
And let her live and die in peace
    Is the end of my song.

SAVING A TRAIN

'Twas in the year of 1869, and on the 19th of November,
Which the people in Southern Germany will long remember,
The great rain-storm which for twenty hours did pour down,
That the rivers were overflowed and petty streams all around.

The rain fell in such torrents as had never been seen before,
That it seemed like a second deluge, the mighty torrents' roar,
At nine o'clock at night the storm did rage and moan,
When Carl Springel set out on his crutches all alone —

From the handsome little hut in which he dwelt,
With some food to his father, for whom he greatly felt,
Who was watching at the railway bridge,
Which was built upon a perpendicular rocky ridge.

The bridge was composed of iron and wooden blocks,
And crossed o'er the Devil's Gulch, an immense cleft of rocks,
Two hundred feet wide and one hundred and fifty feet deep,
And enough to make one's flesh to creep.

Far beneath the bridge a mountain-stream did boil and rumble,
And on that night did madly toss and tumble;
Oh! it must have been an awful sight
To see the great cataract falling from such a height.

It was the duty of Carl's father to watch the bridge on
    stormy nights,
And warn the on-coming trains of danger with the red lights;
So, on this stormy night, the boy Carl hobbled along
Slowly and fearlessly upon his crutches, because he wasn't
    strong.

He struggled on manfully with all his might
Through the fearful darkness of the night,
And half-blinded by the heavy rain,
But still resolved the bridge to gain.

But, when within one hundred yards of the bridge, it gave
    way with an awful crash,
And fell into the roaring flood below, and made a fearful
    splash,
Which rose high above the din of the storm,
The like brave Carl never heard since he was born.

Then father! father! cried Carl in his loudest tone,
Father! father! he shouted again in very pitiful moans;
But no answering voice did reply,
Which caused him to heave a deep-fetched sigh.

And now to brave Carl the truth was clear
That he had lost his father dear,
And he cried, My poor father's lost, and cannot be found
He's gone down with the bridge, and has been drowned.

But he resolves to save the on-coming train,
So every nerve and muscle he does strain,
And he trudges along dauntlessly on his crutches,
And tenaciously to them he clutches.

And just in time he reaches his father's car
To save the on-coming train from afar,
So he seizes the red light, and swings it round,
And cries with all his might, The bridge is down! The
   bridge is down!

So forward his father's car he drives,
Determined to save the passengers' lives,
Struggling hard with might and main,
Hoping his struggle won't prove in vain.

So on comes the iron-horse snorting and rumbling,
And the mountain-torrent at the bridge kept roaring and
      tumbling;
While brave Carl keeps shouting, The bridge is down! The
      bridge is down!
He cried with a pitiful wail and sound.

But, thank heaven, the engine-driver sees the red light
That Carl keeps swinging round his head with all his might;
But bang! bang! goes the engine with a terrible crash,
And the car is dashed all to smash.

But the breaking of the car stops the train,
And poor Carl's struggle is not in vain;
But, poor soul, he was found stark dead,
Crushed and mangled from foot to head!

And the passengers were all loud in Carl's praise,
And from the cold wet ground they did him raise,
And tears for brave Carl fell silently around,
Because he had saved two hundred passengers from being
    drowned.

In a quiet village cemetery he now sleeps among the silent
    dead,
In the south of Germany, with a tombstone at his head,
Erected by the passengers he saved in the train,
And which to his memory will long remain.

THE MOON

Beautiful Moon, with thy silvery light,
Thou seemest most charming to my sight;
As I gaze upon thee in the sky so high,
A tear of joy does moisten mine eye.

Beautiful Moon, with thy silvery light,
Thou cheerest the Esquimau in the night;
For thou lettest him see to harpoon the fish,
And with them he makes a dainty dish.

Beautiful Moon, with thy silvery light,
Thou cheerest the fox in the night,
And lettest him see to steal the grey goose away
Out of the farm-yard from a stack of hay.

Beautiful Moon, with thy silvery light,
Thou cheerest the farmer in the night,
And makest his heart beat high with delight
As he views his crops by the light in the night.

Beautiful Moon, with thy silvery light,
Thou cheerest the eagle in the night,
And lettest him see to devour his prey
And carry it to his nest away.

Beautiful Moon, with thy silvery light,
Thou cheerest the mariner in the night
As he paces the deck alone,
Thinking of his dear friends at home.

Beautiful Moon, with thy silvery light,
Thou cheerest the weary traveller in the night;
For thou lightest up the wayside around
To him when he is homeward bound.

Beautiful Moon, with thy silvery light,
Thou cheerest the lovers in the night
As they walk through the shady groves alone,
Making love to each other before they go home.

Beautiful Moon, with thy silvery light,
Thou cheerest the poacher in the night;
For thou lettest him see to set his snares
To catch the rabbits and the hares.

THE BEAUTIFUL SUN

Beautiful sun! with thy golden rays,
To God, the wise Creator, be all praise;
For thou nourisheth all the creation,
Wherever there is found to be animation.

Without thy heat we could not live,
Then praise to God we ought to give;
For thou makest the fruits and provisions to grow,
To nourish all creatures on earth below.

Thou makest the hearts of the old feel glad,
Likewise the yound child and the lad,
And the face of Nature to look green and gay,
And the little children to sport and play.

Thou also giveth light unto the Moon,
Which certainly is a very great boon
To all God's creatures here below,
Throughtout the world where'er they go.

How beautiful thou look'st on a summer morn,
When thou sheddest thy effulgence among the yellow corn,
Also upon lake, and river, and the mountain tops,
Whilst thou leavest behind the most lovely dewdrops!

How beautiful thou seem'st in the firmament above,
As I gaze upon thee, my heart fills with love
To God, the great Creator, Who has placed thee there,
Who watches all His creatures with an eye of care!

Thou makest the birds to sing on the tree,
Also by meadow, mountain, and lea;
And the lark high poised up in air,
Carolling its little song with its heart free from care.

Thou makest the heart of the shepherd feel gay
As he watches the little lambkins at their innocent play;
While he tends them on the hillside all day,
Taking care that none of them shall go astray.

Thou cheerest the weary traveller while on his way
During the livelong summer day,
As he admires the beautiful scenery while passing along,
And singing to himself a stave of a song.

Thou cheerest the tourist while amongst the Highland hills,
As he views their beautiful sparkling rills
Glittering like diamonds by thy golden rays,
While the hills seem to offer up to God their praise.

While the bee from flower to flower does roam
To gather honey, and carry it home;
While it hums its little song in the beautiful sunshine,
And seemingly to thank the Creator divine—

For the honey it hath gathered during the day,
In the merry month of May,
When the flowers are in full bloom,
Also the sweet honeysuckle and the broom.

How beautiful thy appearance while setting in the west,
Whilst encircled with red and azure, 'tis then thou look'st best!
Then let us all thank God for thy golden light
In our prayers every morning and night!

GRACE DARLING,
OR THE WRECK OF THE "FORFARSHIRE"

As the night was beginning to close in one rough September
    day
In the year of 1838, a steamer passed through the Fairway
Between the Farne Islands and the coast, on her passage
    northwards;
But the wind was against her, and the steamer laboured hard.

There she laboured in the heavy sea against both wind and
    tide,
While a dense fog enveloped her on every side;
And the mighty billows made her timbers creak,
Until at last, unfortunately, she sprung a leak.

Then all hands rushed to the pumps, and wrought with
    might and main.
But the water, alas! alarmingly on them did gain;
And the thick sleet was driving across the raging sea,
While the wind it burst upon them in all its fury.

And the fearful gale and the murky aspect of the sky
Caused the passengers on board to lament and sigh
As the sleet drove thick, furious, and fast,
And as the waves surged mountains high, they stood aghast.

And the screaming of the sea-birds foretold a gathering storm,
And the passengers, poor souls, looked pale and forlorn,
And on every countenance was depicted woe
As the "Forfarshire" steamer was pitched to and fro.

And the engine-fires with the water were washed out;
Then, as the tide set strongly in, it wheeled the vessel about,
And the ill-fated vessel drifted helplessly along;
But the fog cleared up a little as the night wore on.

Then the terror-stricken crew saw the breakers ahead,
And all thought of being saved from them fled;
And the Farne lights were shining hazily through the gloom,
While in the fore-cabin a woman lay with two children in a
    swoon.

Before the morning broke, the "Forfarshire" struck upon a
    rock,
And was dashed to pieces by a tempestuous shock,
Which raised her for a moment, and dashed her down again,
Then the ill-starred vessel was swallowed up in the briny main.

Before the vessel broke up, some nine or ten of the crew intent
To save their lives, or perish in the attempt,
Lowered one of the boats while exhausted and forlorn,
And, poor souls, were soon lost sight of in the storm.

Around the windlass on the forecastle some dozen poor
    wretches clung,
And with despair and grief their weakly hearts were rung
As the merciless sea broke o'er them every moment;
But God in His mercy to them Grace Darling sent.

By the first streak of dawn she early up had been,
And happened to look out upon the stormy scene,
And she descried the wreck through the morning gloom;
But she resolved to rescue them from such a perilous doom.

Then she cried, Oh! father dear, come here and see the wreck,
See, here take the telescope, and you can inspect;
Oh! father, try and save them, and heaven will you bless;
But, my darling, no help can reach them in such a storm as this.

Oh! my kind father, you will surely try and save
These poor souls from a cold and watery grave;
Oh! I cannot sit to see them perish before mine eyes,
And, for the love of heaven, do not my pleading despise!

Then old Darling yielded, and launched the little boat,
And high on the big waves the boat did float;
Then Grace and her father took each an oar in hand,
And to see Grace Darling rowing the picture was grand.

And as the little boat to the sufferers drew near,
Poor souls, they tried to raise a cheer;
But as they gazed upon the heroic Grace,
The big tears trickled down each sufferer's face.

And nine persons were rescued almost dead with the cold
By modest and lovely Grace Darling, that heroine bold;
The survivors were taken to the light-house, and remained
     there two days,
And every one of them was loud in Grace Darling's praise.

Grace Darling was a comely lass, with long, fair floating hair,
With soft blue eyes, and shy, and modesty rare;
And her countenance was full of sense and genuine kindliness,
With a noble heart, and ready to help suffering creatures in
     distress.

But, alas! three years after her famous exploit,
Which, to the end of time, will never be forgot,
Consumption, that fell destroyer, carried her away
To heaven, I hope, to be an angel for ever and aye.

Before she died, scores of suitors in marriage sought her hand;
But no, she'd rather live in Longstone light-house on Farne
     island,
And there she lived and died with her father and mother,
And for her equal in true heroism we cannot find another.

ADVENTURE IN THE LIFE OF
KING JAMES V OF SCOTLAND

On one occasion King James the Fifth of Scotland, when
    alone, in disguise,
Near by the Bridge of Cramond met with rather a disagreeable
    surprise.
He was attacked by five gipsy men without uttering a word,
But he manfully defended himself with his sword.

There chanced to be a poor man threshing corn in a barn
    near by,
Who came out on hearing the noise so high;
And seeing one man defending himself so gallantly,
That he attacked the gipsies with his flail, and made them flee

Then he took the King into the barn,
Saying, "I hope, sir, you've met with no great harm;
And for five men to attack you, it's a disgrace;
But stay, I'll fetch a towel and water to wash your face."

And when the King washed the blood off his face and hands,
"Now, sir, I wish to know who you are," the King demands.
"My name, sir, is John Howieson, a bondsman on the farm
    of Braehead."
"Oh, well," replied the King, "your company I need not
    dread."

"And perhaps you'll accompany me a little way towards
    Edinburgh,
Because at present I'm not free from sorrow.
And if you have any particular wish to have gratified,
Let me know it, and it shall not be denied."

Then honest John said, thinking it no harm,
"Sir, I would like to be the owner of Braehead farm;
But by letting me know who you are it would give my mind
    relief."
Then King James he answered that he was the Gudeman of
    Ballingeich.

"And if you'll meet me at the palace on next Sunday,
Believe me, for your manful assistance, I'll you repay.
Nay, honest John, don't think of you I'm making sport,
I pledge my word at least you shall see the royal court."

So on the next Sunday John put on his best clothes,
And appeared at the palace gate as you may suppose.
And he inquired for the Gudeman of Ballingeich;
And when he gained admittance his heart was freed from
    grief.

For John soon found his friend the Gudeman,
And the King took John by the han',
Then conducted John from one apartment to another,
Just as kindly as if he'd been his own brother.

Then the King asked John if he'd like to see His Majesty.
"Oh, yes," replied John, "His Majesty I would really like
    to see."
And John looked earnestly into the King's face,
And said, "How am I to know His Grace?"

"Oh, John, you needn't be the least annoyed about that,
For all heads will be uncovered: the King will wear his hat."
Then he conducted John into a large hall,
Which was filled by the nobility, crown officers, and all.

Then said John to the King, when he looked round the room,
"Sir, I hope I will see the King very soon,"
Because to see the King, John rather dreaded,
At last he said to the King, "'Tis you! the rest are bare-headed."

Then the King said, "John, I give you Braehead farm as it
    stands,
On condition you provide a towel and basin of water to wash
    my hands,
If ever I chance to come your way."
Then John said, "Thanks to your Majesty, I'll willingly obey."

THE CLEPINGTON CATASTROPHE

'Twas on a Monday morning, and in the year of 1884,
That a fire broke out in Bailie Bradford's store,
Which contained bales of jute and large quantities of waste,
Which the brave firemen ran to extinguish in great haste.

They left their wives that morning without any dread,
Never thinking, at the burning pile, they would be killed dead
By the falling of the rickety and insecure walls;
When I think of it, kind Christians, my heart it appals!

Because it has caused widows and their families to shed briny
    tears,
For there hasn't been such a destructive fire for many years;
Whereby four brave firemen have perished in the fire,
And for better fathers or husbands no family could desire.

'Twas about five o'clock in the morning the fire did break out,
While one of the workmen was inspecting the premises round
    about—
Luckily before any one had begun their work for the day—
So he instantly gave the alarm without delay.

At that time only a few persons were gathered on the spot,
But in a few minutes some hundreds were got,
Who came flying in all directions, and in great dismay;
So they help'd to put out the fire without delay.

But the spreading flames, within the second flats, soon began
    to appear,
Which filled the spectators' hearts with sympathy and
    fear,
Lest any one should lose their life in the merciless fire,
When they saw it bursting out and ascending higher and
    higher.

Captain Ramsay, of the Dundee Fire Brigade, was the first
    to arrive,
And under his directions the men seemed all alive,
For they did their work heroically, with all their might and
    main,
In the midst of blinding smoke and the burning flame.

As soon as the catastrophe came to be known,
The words, Fire! Fire! from every mouth were blown;
And a cry of despair rang out on the morning air,
When they saw the burning pile with its red fiery glare.

While a dense cloud of smoke seemed to darken the sky,
And the red glaring flame ascended up on high,
Which made the scene appear weird-like around;
While from the spectators was heard a murmuring sound.

But the brave firemen did their duty manfully to the last,
And plied the water on the burning pile, copiously and fast;
But in a moment, without warning, the front wall gave way,
Which filled the people's hearts with horror and dismay:

Because four brave firemen were killed instantaneously on
   the spot,
Which by the spectators will never be forgot;
While the Fire Fiend laughingly did hiss and roar,
As he viewed their mangled bodies, with the *debris* covered
   o'er.

But in the midst of dust and fire they did their duty well,
Aye! in the midst of a shower of bricks falling on them
   pell-mell,
Until they were compelled to let the water-hose go;
While the blood from their bruised heads and arms did flow.

But brave James Fyffe held on to the hose until the last,
And when found in the *debris,* the people stood aghast.
When they saw him lying dead, with the hose in his hand,
Their tears for him they couldn't check nor yet command.

Oh, heaven! I must confess it was no joke
To see them struggling in the midst of suffocating smoke,
Each man struggling hard, no doubt, to save his life,
When he thought of his dear children and his wife.

But still the merciless flame shot up higher and higher;
Oh, God! it is terrible and cruel to perish by fire;
Alas! it was saddening and fearful to behold,
When I think of it, kind Christians, it makes my blood run
   cold.

What makes the death of Fyffe the more distressing,
He was going to be the groomsman at his sister's bridal
   dressing,
Who was going to be married the next day;
But, alas! the brave hero's life was taken away.

But accidents will happen by land and by sea,
Therefore, to save ourselves from accidents, we needn't try
   to flee,
For whatsoever God has ordained will come to pass;
For instance, ye may be killed by a stone or a piece of glass.

I hope the Lord will provide for the widows in their distress,
For they are to be pitied, I really must confess;
And I hope the public of Dundee will lend them a helping
   hand;
To help the widows and the fatherless is God's command.

THE REBEL SURPRISE NEAR TAMAI

'Twas on the 22nd of March, in the year 1885,
That the Arabs rushed like a mountain torrent in full drive,
And quickly attacked General M'Neill's transport-zereba,
But in a short time they were forced to withdraw.

And in the suddenness of surprise the men were carried away,
Also camels, mules, and horses were thrown into wild
   disarray,
By thousands of the Arabs that in ambush lay,
But our brave British heroes held the enemy at bay.

There was a multitude of camels heaped upon one another,
Kicking and screaming, while many of them did smother,
Owing to the heavy pressure of the entangled mass,
That were tramping o'er one another as they lay on the grass.

The scene was indescribable, and sickening to behold,
To see the mass of innocent brutes lying stiff and cold,
And the moaning cries of them were pitiful to hear,
Likewise the cries of the dying men that lay wounded in the
   rear.

Then General M'Neill ordered his men to form in solid square,
Whilst deafening shouts and shrieks of animals did rend the
air,
And the rush of stampeded camels made a fearful din,
While the Arabs they did yell, and fiendishly did grin.

Then the gallant Marines formed the east side of the square,
While clouds of dust and smoke did darken the air,
And on the west side the Berkshire were engaged in the fight,
Firing steadily and coolly with all their might.

Still camp followers were carried along by the huge animal
mass,
And along the face of the zereba 'twas difficult to pass,
Because the mass of brutes swept on in wild dismay,
Which caused the troops to be thrown into disorderly array.

Then Indians and Bluejackets were all mixed together back
to back,
And for half-an-hour the fire and din didn't slack;
And none but steady troops could have stood that fearful shock,
Because against overwhelming numbers they stood as firm
as a rock.

The Arabs crept among the legs of the animals without any
dread.
But by the British bullets many were killed dead,
And left dead on the field and weltering in their gore,
Whilst the dying moans of the camels made a hideous roar.

Then General M'Neill to his men did say,
Forward! my lads, and keep them at bay!
Come, make ready, my men, and stand to your arms,
And don't be afraid of war's alarms!

So forward! and charge them in front and rear,
And remember you are fighting for you Queen and country
    dear,
Therefore, charge them with your bayonets, left and right,
And we'll soon put this rebel horde to flight.

Then forward at the bayonet-charge they did rush,
And the rebel horde they soon did crush;
And by the charge of the bayonet they kept them at bay,
And in confusion and terror they all fled away.

The Marines held their own while engaged hand-to-hand,
And the courage they displayed was really very grand;
But it would be unfair to praise one corps more than
    another,
Because each man fought as if he'd been avenging the death
    of a brother.

The Berkshire men and the Naval Brigade fought with
    might and main,
And, thank God! the British have defeated the Arabs once
    again,
And have added fresh laurels to their name,
Which will be enrolled in the book of fame.

'Tis lamentable to think of the horrors of war,
That men must leave their homes and go abroad afar,
To fight for their Queen and country in a foreign land,
Beneath the whirlwind's drifting scorching sand.

But whatsoever God wills must come to pass,
The fall of a sparrow, or a tiny blade of grass;
Also, man must fall at home by His command,
Just equally the same as in a foreign land.

THE BATTLE OF CRESSY

'Twas on the 26th of August, the sun was burning hot,
In the year of 1346, which will never be forgot,
Because the famous field of Cressy was slippery and gory,
By the loss of innocent blood which I'll relate in story.

To the field of Cressy boldly King philip did advance,
Aided by the Bohemian Army and chosen men of France,
And treble the strength of the English Army that day,
But the lance thrusts of the English soon made them give
    way.

The English Army was under the command of the Prince of
    Wales,
And with ringing cheers the soldiers his presence gladly hails,
As King Edward spoke to the Prince, his son, and said,
My son put thou thy trust in God and be not afraid,
And be will protect thee in the midst of the fight,
And remember God always defends the right.

Then the Prince knelt on one knee before the King.
Whilst the soldiers gathered round them in a ring;
Then the King commanded that the Prince should be
    carefully guarded,
And if they were victorious each man would be rewarded.

These arrangements being made, the Prince rode away,
And as he rode past the ranks, his spirits felt gay;
Then he ordered the men to refresh themselves without
    delay,
And prepare to meet the enemy in the coming deadly fray.

Then contentedly the men seated themselves upon the grass,
And ate and drank to their hearts content, until an hour did
  pass;
Meanwhile the French troops did advance in disorganised
  masses,
But as soon as the English saw them they threw aside their
  glasses.

And they rose and stood in the ranks as solid as the rock,
All ready and eager to receive the enemy's shock;
And as the morning was advancing a little beyond noon,
They all felt anxious for the fight, likewise to know their doom.

Then the French considered they were unable to begin the
  attack,
And seemed rather inclined for to draw back;
But Count D'Alencon ordered them on to the attack,
Then the rain poured down in torrents and the thunder did
  crack.

Then forward marched the French with mock shrill cries,
But the English their cries most bravely defies;
And as the sun shone out in all its brilliant array,
The English let fly their arrows at them without the least
  dismay.

And each man fought hard with sword and lance pell mell,
And the ranks were instantly filled up as soon as a man fell;
And the Count D'Alencon, boldly charged the Black Prince.
And he cried, yield you, Sir Knight, or I'll make you wince.

Ha, by St George! thou knowest not what thou sayest,
Therefore yield thyself, Sir Frenchman, for like an ass thou
  brayest;
Then planting his lance he ran at the Count without fear,
And the Count fell beneath the Black Prince's spear.

And the Black Prince and his men fought right manfully,
By this time against some forty thousand of the enemy,
Until the Prince recognised the banner of Bohemia floating in
    the air;
Then he cried that banner shall be mine, by St George
    I do swear.

On! on! for old England, he cried, on! gentlemen on!
And spur your chargers quickly, and after them begone;
Then the foremost, a slight youth, to the Prince did reply,
My Prince I'll capture that banner for you else I will die

Ha! cried the Prince, is it thou my gallant Jack of Kent,
Now charge with me my brave lad for thou has been sent
By God, to aid me in the midst of the fight,
So forward, and wield your cudgel with all your might.

Then right into the midst of the Bohemian Knights they
    fought their way,
Brave Jack o' the Cudgel and the Prince without dismay;
And Jack rushed at the Standard Bearer without any dread,
And struck him a blow with his cudgel which killed him dead.

Then Jack bore off the Standard, to the Prince's delight,
Then the French and the Bohemians instantly took to flight;
And as the last rays of the sun had faded in the west,
The wounded and dying on both sides longed for rest.

And Philip, King of France, was wounded twice in the fray,
And was forced to fly from the field in great dismay;
And John of Hainault cried, come sire, come away,
I hope you will live to win some other day.

Then King Edward and his army, and the Prince his son,
Knelt down and thanked God for the victory won;
And the King's heart was filled with great delight,
And he thanked jack for capturing the Bohemian Standard
    during the fight.

WRECK OF THE BARQUE "WM. PATERSON"
OF LIVERPOOL

Ye landsmen all attend my verse, and I'll tell to ye a tale
Concerning the barque "Wm. Paterson" that was lost in a
    tempestuous gale?"
She was on a voyage from Bangkok to the Clyde with a cargo
    of Teakwood,
And the crew numbered fifteen in all of seamen firm and good.

'Twas on the 8th of March, when a violent gale from the
    southward broke out,
And for nine days during tempestuous weather their ship was
    tossed about
By the angry sea, and the barque she sprang a leak,
Still the crew wrought at the pumps till their hearts were like
    to break.

And the pumps were kept constantly going for fourteen long
    hours,
And the poor men were drenched to the skin with sea spray showers;
Still they wrought at the pumps till they became rather clogged
Until at last the barque became thoroughly water-logged.

Oh! hard was the fate of these brave men,
While the water did rush in from stern to stem,
Poor souls 'twas enough to have driven them frantic,
To be drifting about water-logged in the Atlantic.

At last she became unmanageable and her masts had to be
    cut away,
Which the brave crew performed quickly without delay;
Still gales of more or less violence prevailed every day,
Whilst the big waves kept dashing o'er them, likewise the
    spray.

And with the fearful hurricane the deckhouse and galley
    were carried away,
Yet the thought of a speedy deliverance kept up their courage
    day by day,
And the captain prepared for the breaking up of the ship
    without dismay,
And to save his rations he reduced each man to two biscuits a
    day.

The brave heroes managed to save a pinnace about fifteen
    feet long,
And into it thirteen of the crew quickly and cautiously did
    throng,
With two bags of biscuits and a cask of water out of the tank,
And for these precious mercies, God they did thank;

Who is the giver of all good things,
And to those that put their trust in him often succour brings,
And such has been the case with these brave men at sea,
That sent Captain M'Mullan to save them and bring them to
    Dundee.

When once into the pinnace they improvised a sail into a tent,
Which to the crew some little shelter lent;
Still every day they were drifting towards the coast of
    Greenland,
Yet they hoped in God that speedy deliverance might be
    near at hand.

And as every day passed by they felt woe begone,
Because no sail could they see on the horizon;
And they constructed a sea anchor to keep the boat's head to
    sea,
Andnotwithstanding their hardships they stood out bravely

And on the 19th of March a ship hove in sight,
Which proved to be the "Slieve Roe" to their delight;
Then they hoisted a signal of distress when they espied the
    "Slieve Roe,"
But it was not seen on account of the wreck being in the
    water so low.

But as soon as Captain M'Mullan knew it was a signal of
    distress,
Then heroically and quickly his men he did address,
He cried! come my men keep the ship close to the wind,
And let's try if we can these unfortunate souls find.

And as the "Slieve Roe" to them drew near,
Poor souls they gave a hearty cheer;
Then they were immediately taken on board,
And they thanked Captain M'Mullan for saving them,
    likewise the Lord.

Then a crew from the "Slieve Roe" were sent away,
For the two remaining members of the crew without delay;
The Captain and a Sailor, together with a cat and a pet dog,
Which had been the companions of the sailors, and seemed as
    frisky as a frog.

And when they had all got safe on board,
With one accord they thanked the Lord;
And Captain M'Mullan kindly did them treat,
By giving them dry clothing and plenty of meat.

And for his kind treatment unto them he deserves great
    praise,
For his many manly and kindly ways,
By saving so many lives during the time he has been at sea,
And in particular for fetching the crew of the "Wm. Paterson"
    safe to Dundee

SORROWS OF THE BLIND

Pity the sorrows of the poor blind,
For they can but little comfort find;
As they walk along the street,
They know not where to put their feet.
They are deprived of that earthly joy
Of seeing either man, woman, or boy;
Sad and lonely through the world they go,
Not knowing a friend from a foe:
Nor the difference betwixt day and night,
For the want of their eyesight;
The blind mother cannot see her darling boy,
That was once her soul's joy.
By day and night,
Since she lost her precious sight;
To her the world seems dark and drear,
And she can find no comfort here.
She once found pleasure in reading books,
But now pale and carewoan are her looks.
Since she has lost her eyesight,
Everything seems wrong and nothing right.

The face of nature, with all its beauties and livery green
Appears to the blind just like a dream.
All things beautiful have vanished from their sight,
Which were once their heart's delight.
The blind father cannot see his beautiful child, nor wife,
That was once the joy of his life;
That he was wont to see at morn and night,
When he had his eyesight.
All comfort has vanished from him now,
And a dejected look hangs on his brow.

Kind Christians all, both great and small,
Pity the sorrows of the blind,
They can but little comfort find;
Therefore we ought to be content with our lot,
And for the eyesight we have got,
And pray to God both day and night
To preserve our eyesight;
And be always willing to help the blind in their distress,
And the Lord will surely bless
And guard us by night and day,
And remember us at the judgement day.

GENERAL GORDON,
THE HERO OF KHARTOUM

ALAS! now o'er the civilised world there hangs a gloom
For brave General Gordon, that was killed in Khartoum;
He was a Christian hero, and a soldier of the Cross,
And to England his death will be a very great loss.

He was very cool in temper, generous and brave,
The friend of the poor, the sick, and the slave;
And many a poor boy he did educate,
And laboured hard to do so both early and late.

He was a man that did not care for worldly gear,
Because the living and true God he did fear;
And the hearts of the poor he liked to cheer,
And by his companions in arms he was loved most dear.

He always took the Bible for his guide,
And he liked little boys to walk by his side;
He preferred their company more so than men,
Because he knew there was less guile in them.

And in his conversation he was modest and plain,
Denouncing all pleasures he considered sinful and vain,
And in battle he carried no weapon but a small cane,
Whilst the bullets fell around him like a shower of rain.

He burnt the debtors' books that were imprisoned in
    Khartoum,
And freed them from a dismal prison gloom,
Those that were imprisoned for debt they couldn't pay,
And sent them rejoicing on their way.

While engaged in the Russian war, in the midst of the fight,
He stood upon a rising ground and viewed them left and right,
But for their shot and shell he didn't care a jot,
While the officers cried, Gordon, come down, or else you'll be
    shot.

His cane was christened by the soldiers Gordon's wand of
    victory,
And when he waved it the soldiers' hearts were filled with
    glee,
While with voice and gesture he encouraged them in the strire,
And he himself appeared to possess a charmed life.

Once when leading a storming party the soldiers drew back,
But he quickly observed that courage they did lack,
Then he calmly lighted a cigar, and turned cheerfully round,
And the soldiers rushed boldly on with a bound.

And they carried the position without delay,
And the Chinese rebels soon gave way,
Because God was with him during the day,
And with those that trust Him for ever and aye.

He was always willing to conduct meetings for the poor,
Also meat and clothing for them he tried to procure,
And he always had little humorous speeches at command,
And to hear him deliver them it must have been grand.

In military life his equal couldn't be found,
No! if you were to search the wide world around,
And 'tis pitiful to think he has met with such a doom
By a base *traitor knave* while in Khartoum.

Yes, the black-hearted traitor opened the gates of Khartoum,
And through that the Christian hero has met his doom,
For when the gates were opened the Arabs rushed madly in,
And foully murdered him while they laughingly did grin.

But he defended himself nobly with axe and sword in hand,
But, alas! he was soon overpowered by that savage band,
And his body received a hundred spear wounds and more,
While his murderers exultingly did loudly shriek and roar.

But heaven's will, 'tis said, must be done,
And according to his own opinion his time was come;
But I hope he is now in heaven reaping his reward.
Although his fate on earth was really very hard.

I hope the people will his memory revere,
And take an example from him, and worship God in fear,
And never be too fond of worldly gear,
And walk in General Gordon's footsteps while they are here.

BURNING OF THE EXETER THEATRE

'Twas in the year of 1887, which many people will long
    remember,
The burning of the Theatre at Exeter on the 5th of September,
Alas! that ever-to-be-remembered and unlucky night,
When one hundred and fifty lost their lives, a most agonising
    sight.

The play on this night was called "Romany Rye,"
And at act four, scene third, Fire! Fire! was the cry;
And all in a moment flames were seen issuing from the stage,
Then the women screamed frantically, like wild beasts in a
    cage.

Then a panic ensued, and each one felt dismayed,
And from the burning building a rush was made;
And soon the theatre was filled with a blinding smoke,
So that the people their way out had to grope.

The shrieks of those trying to escape were fearful to hear,
Especially the cries of those who had lost their friends most
    dear;
Oh, the scene was most painful in the London Inn Square,
To see them ringing their hands and tearing their hair!

And as the flames spread, great havoc they did make,
And the poor souls fought heroically in trying to make their
    escape;
Oh, it was horrible to see men and women trying to reach the
    door!
But in many cases death claimed the victory, and their
    struggles were o'er.

Alas! 't was pitiful the shrieks of the audience to hear,
Especially as the flames to them drew near;
Because on every face were depicted despair and woe,
And many of them jumped from the windows into the street
below.

The crushed and charred bodies were carried into London
Hotel yard,
And to alleviate their sufferings the doctors tried hard;
But, alas! their attendance on many was thrown away,
But those that survived were conveyed to Exeter Hospital
without delay.

And all those that had their wounds dressed proceeded home,
Accompanied by their friends, and making a loud moan;
While the faces and necks of others were sickening to behold,
Enough to chill one's blood, and make the heart turn cold,

Alas! words fail to describe the desolation,
And in many homes it will cause great lamentation;
Because human remains are beyond all identification,
Which will cause the relatives of the sufferers' to be in great
tribulation.

Oh, Heaven! it must have been an awful sight,
To see the poor souls struggling hard with all their might,
Fighting hard their lives to save,
While many in the smoke and burning flame did madly rave!

It was the most sickening sight that ever anybody saw,
Human remains, beyond recognition, covered with a heap of
straw;
And here and there a body might be seen, and a maimed
hand,
Oh, such a sight, that the most hard-hearted person could
hardly withstand!

The number of the people in the theatre was between seven
   and eight thousand,
But, alas! one hundred and fifty by the fire have been found
   dead;
And the most lives were lost on the stairs leading from the
   gallery,
And these were roasted to death, which was sickening to see.

The funerals were conducted at the expense of the local
   authority,
And two hours and more elapsed at the mournful ceremony;
And at one grave there were two thousand people, a very
   great crowd,
And most of the men were bareheaded and weeping aloud.

Alas! many poor children have been bereft of their fathers
   and mothers,
Who will be sorely missed by little sisters and brothers;
But, alas! unto them they can ne'er return again,
Therefore the poor little innocents must weep for them in vain.

I hope all kind Christian souls will help the friends of the dead,
Especially those that have lost the winners of their bread;
and if they do, God surely will them bless,
Because pure Christianity is to help the widows and orphans
   in distress.

I am very glad to see Henry Irving has sent a hundred
   pound,
And I hope his brother actors will subscribe their mite all
   round;
And if they do it will add honour to their name,
Because whatever is given towards a good cause they will it
   regain.

JOHN ROUAT THE FISHERMAN

Margaret Simpson was the daughter of humble parents in
   the county of Ayr,
With a comely figure, and face of beauty rare,
And just in the full bloom of her womanhood
Was united to John Rouat, a fisherman good.

John's fortune consisted of his coble, three cars, and his
   fishing-gear,
Besides his two stout boys, John and James, he loved most
   dear.
And no matter how the wind might blow, or the rain pelt,
Or scarcity of fish, John little sorrow felt.

While sitting by the clear blazing hearth of his home,
With beaming faces around it, all his own.
But John, the oldest son, refused his father obedience,
Which John Rouat considered a most grievous offence.

So his father tried to check him, but all wouldn't do,
And John joined a revenue cutter as one of its crew;
And when his father heard it he bitterly did moan,
And angrily forbade him never to return home.

Then shortly after James ran away to sea without his
   parents' leave,
So John Rouat became morose, and sadly did grieve.
But one day he received a letter, stating his son John was
   dead,
And when he read the sad news all comfort from him fled.

Then shortly after that his son James was shot,
For allowing a deserter to escape, such was his lot;
And through the death of his two sons he felt dejected,
And the condolence of kind neighbours by him was rejected.

'Twas near the close of autumn, when one day the sky
    became o'ercast,
And John Rouat, contrary to his wife's will, went to sea at
    last,
When suddenly the sea began to roar, and angry billows
    swept along,
And, alas! the stormy tempest for John Rouat proved too
    strong.

But still he clutched the oars, thinking to keep his coble
    afloat,
When one 'whelming billow struck heavily against the boat,
And man and boat were engulfed in the briny wave,
While the Storm Fiend did roar and madly did rave.

When Margaret Rouat heard of her husband's loss, her
    sorrow was very great,
And the villagers of Bute were moved with pity for her sad
    fate,
And for many days and nights she wandered among the
    hills,
Lamenting the loss of her husband and other ills.

Until worn out by fatigue, towards a ruinous hut she did
    creep,
And there she lay down on the earthen floor, and fell
    asleep,
And as a herd boy by chance was passing by,
He looked into the hut and the body of Margaret he did espy.

Then the herd boy fled to communicate his fears,
And the hut was soon filled with villagers, and some shed
    tears.
When they discovered in the unhappy being they had found
Margaret Rouat, their old neighbour, then their sorrow was
    profound.

Then the men from the village of Bute willingly lent their aid,
To patch up the miserable hut, and great attention to her
    was paid.
And Margaret Rouat lived there in solitude for many years,
Although at times the simple creature shed many tears.

Margaret was always willing to work for her bread,
Sometimes she herded cows without any dread,
Besides sometimes she was allowed to ring the parish bell,
And for doing so she was always paid right well.

In an old box she kept her money hid away,
But being at the kirk one beautiful Sabbath day,
When to her utter dismay when she returned home,
She found the bottom forced from the box, and the money gone.

Then she wept like a child, in a hysteric fit,
Regarding the loss of her money, and didn't very long
    survive it.
And as she was wont to descend to the village twice a week,
The villagers missed her, and resolved they would for her
    seek.

Then two men from the village, on the next day
Sauntered up to her dwelling, and to their dismay,
They found the door half open, and one stale crust of bread,
And on a rude pallet lay poor Margaret Rouat cold and dead.

HANCHEN, THE MAID OF THE MILL

NEAR the village of Udorf, on the banks of the Rhine,
There lived a miller and his family, once on a time;
And there yet stands the mill in a state of decay,
And concerning the miller and his family, attend to my lay

The miller and his family went to Church one Sunday morn,
Leaving behind their darling child, the youngest born,
In charge of brave Hanchen, the servant maid,
A kind-hearted girl and not the least afraid.

As Hanchen was engaged preparing dinner for the family
She chanced to turn round, and there she did see
Heinrich Bottler, her lover, and she sincerely loved him,
Then she instantly got him something to eat and bade him
    begin.

And in the midst of her business she sat down beside him,
While he did justice to the meat and thought it no sin,
But while he was eating he let fall his knife,
Then he commanded Hanchen to pick it up or else he'd take
    her life.

Then as she stooped down to pick up the knife,
The villain caught her by the throat, and swore he'd take her
    life,
Then he drew a dagger from under his coat,
Crying tell me where your master's money is, or I'll cut your
    throat

And still he threatened to kill her with the dagger in his hand,
If the poor girl didn't comply with his demand,
While in his choking grasp her breath was fleeting faster and
    faster,
Therefore she had no other choice but to die or betray her
    master.

Then she cried, mercy, for Heaven's sake let go thy hold,
And I'll tell thee where my master keeps his gold;
Then he let go his hold without delay,
And she unto him thus boldly did say.

Here, take this axe and use it, while I run upstairs,
To gather all my money, besides all my wares,
Because I'm resolved to fly along with you,
When you've robbed my master of his gold and bid France
    adieu.

Then deceived by her plan he allowed her to leave the room,
Telling her to make haste and come back very soon,
Then to her master's bedroom she led the way,
And showed him the coffer where her master's money lay.

Then Heinrich with the axe broke the coffer very soon,
While Hanchen instead of going upstairs to her room,
Bolted all the doors upon him without dismay,
While Heinrich was busy preparing to carry her master's
    money away.

Then she rushed to the mill to give the alarm,
Resolved to protect her master's money, while she could
    wield an arm;
And the only being in sight, was her master's boy of five
    years old,
Then she cried, run! run! and tell father there's a robber
    taking his gold.

Then the boy did as she bid him without any doubt,
And set off, running on the road she pointed out;
But at this moment, a shrill whistle made her stand aghast,
When she heard Heinrich, crying, catch that child that's
   running so fast.

But still the boy ran on with might and main,
Until a ruffian sprang up from the bed of a natural drain;
And snatching the boy in his arms, and hastening towards
   the mill,
While brave Hanchen was afraid the boy he would kill.

Then the villain came rushing with the boy towards the mill,
Crying, open the door, or the child I'll kill;
But she cried, never will I open the door to thee,
No! I will put my trust in God, and He'll save the child and me.

Then the ruffian set down the child, for a moment to look
   about,
Crying, open the door, or I'll fire the mill without doubt;
And while searching for combustibles, he discovered an inlet
   to the mill,
Saying, my pretty maid, once I get in, it's you I will kill.

Then he tied the hands and feet of the poor child,
Which caused it to scream with fear, very wild;
Then he stole back to the aperture to effect an entrance,
And when Hanchen saw him, she said now is my chance.

So the ruffian got safely in the great drum wheel,
Then Hanchen set on the engine, which made the ruffian reel;
And as he was whirled about, he screamed aloud,
And when Hanchen saw him like a rat in a trap, she felt very
   proud.

At length the master arrived and his family,
And when she heard his kindly voice her heart was full of glee,
Then she opened the mill door and let him in,
While her eyes with tears of joy were full to the brim.

Then the master set off the engine without delay,
And the ruffian was dragged forth while he shook with
    dismay,
And Heinrich and he were bound together under a strong
    escort,
And conveyed to Bonn Prison where villains resort.

So thus ends the story of Hanchen, a heroine brave,
That tried hard her master's gold to save,
And for her bravery she got married to the miller's eldest son,
And Hanchen on her marriage night cried Heaven's will be
    done.

WRECK OF THE SCHOONER "SAMUEL CRAWFORD"

'Twas in the year of 1886, and on the 29th of November,
Which the surviving crew of the "Samuel Crawford" will
    long remember,
She was bound to Baltimore with a cargo of pine lumber;
But, alas! the crew suffered greatly from cold and hunger.

'Twas on December 3rd when about ten miles south-west
Of Currituck light, and scudding at her best;
That a heavy gale struck her a merciless blow,
Which filled the hearts of the crew with fear and woe.

Then the merciless snow came down, hiding everything from
    view,
And as the night closed in the wind tempestuous blew;
Still the brave crew reefed the spanker and all the sails,
While not one amongst them with fear bewails.

Still the gallant little schooner ploughed on the seas,
Through the blinding snow and the stormy breeze;
Until it increased to a fearful hurricane,
Yet the crew wrought manfully and didn't complain.

But during the night the wind it harder blew,
And the brave little schooner was hove to;
And on the morning of December the 4th the wind died
    out,
But it rent the schooner from stem to stern without any
    doubt.

And the seas were running mountains high,
While the poor sailors, no doubt, heaved many a sigh;
Because they must have felt cold, and the schooner sprung a
    leak,
Still they wrought while their hearts were like to break.

Then the wind it sprang up in terrific fury again,
But the crew baled out the water with might and main;
But still the water fast on them did gain,
Yet the brave heroes disdained to complain.

On the morning of December the 4th she was scudding before
    a hurricane,
And the crew were exhausted, but managed the poop to gain;
And the vessel was tossed like a cork on the wave,
While the brave crew expected to meet with a watery grave.

And huge beams and pine planks were washed overboard,
While Captain Tilton looked on and said never a word;
And the crew likewise felt quite content,
Until the fore-and-aft rigging overboard went.

Then loudly for help to God they did cry,
And to their earnest prayer He did draw nigh;
And saved them from a watery grave,
When help from Him they did crave.

Poor souls they expected to be engulfed every hour,
And to appease their hunger they made dough with salt
    water and flour;
And made a sort of hard cake placed over a griddle hole,
To satisfy their hunger, which, alas! is hard to thole.

And two of these cakes each man got per day,
Which the poor creatures devoured in a ravenous way;
Along with a little fresh water to wash it down,
Which they most thankfully praised God for and didn't
    frown.

And on the 10th of December when they had burned their
    last light,
The ship "Orinoco" bound for New York hove in sight;
And they were rescued safely and taken on board,
And they thanked the Captain, and likewise the Lord.

Then the Captain of the "Orinoco" ordered her to be set
    on fire,
Which was quickly done as he did desire;
Which caused the rescued crew to stare in amaze,
And to take the last look of their schooner in a blaze.

THE FIRST GRENADIER OF FRANCE

'Twas in a certain regiment of French Grenadiers,
A touching and beautiful custom was observed many years;
Which was meant to commemorate the heroism of a departed
comrade,
And when the companies assembled for parade,
There was one name at roll call to which no answer was made.

It was that of the noble La Tour d'Auvergne,
The first Grenadier of France, heroic and stern;
And always at roll call the oldest sergeant stepped forward a
pace,
And loudly cried, "died on the field of battle," then fell back
into his place.

He always refused offers of high promotion,
Because to be promoted from the ranks he had no notion;
But at last he was in command of eight thousand men,
Hence he was called the first Grenadier of France, La Tour
d'Auvergne.

When forty years of age he went on a visit to a friend,
Never thinking he would have a French garrison to defend
And while there he made himself acquainted with the country,
But the war had shifted to that quarter unfortunately.

But although the war was there he felt undaunted,
Because to fight on behalf of France was all he wanted;
And the thought thereof did his mind harass,
When he knew a regiment of Austrians was pushing on to
occupy a narrow pass.

They were pushing on in hot haste and no delaying,
And only two hours distant from where the Grenadier was
staying,
But when he knew he set off at once for the pass,
Determined if 'twere possible the enemy to harass.

He knew that the pass was defended by a stout tower,
And to destroy the garrison the enemy would exert all their
  power;
But he hoped to be able to warn the French of their danger,
But to the thirty men garrisoned there he was quite a
  stranger.

Still the brave hero hastened on, and when he came there,
He found the thirty men had fled in wild despair;
Leaving their thirty muskets behind,
But to defend the garrison to the last he made up his mind.

And in searching he found several boxes of ammunition not
  destroyed,
And for a moment he felt a little annoyed;
Then he fastened the main door, with the articles he did find,
And when he had done so he felt satisfied in mind.

Then he ate heartily of the provisions he had brought,
And waited patiently for the enemy, absorbed in thought;
And formed the heroic resolution to defend the tower,
Alone, against the enemy, while he had the power.

There the brave hero sat alone quite content,
Resolved to hold the garrison, or die in the attempt;
And about midnight his practised ear caught the tramp of
  feet,
But he had everything ready for the attack and complete.

There he sat and his mind absorbed in deep distress,
But he discharged a couple of muskets into the darkness;
To warn the enemy that he knew they were there,
Then he heard the Austrian officers telling their men to
  beware.

So until morning he was left unmolested,
And quietly till daylight the brave Grenadier rested;
But at sunrise the Austrian commander called on the garrison
to surrender,
But the Grenadier replied, "never, I am its sole defender."

Then a piece of artillery was brought to bear upon the tower,
But the Grenadier from his big gun rapid fire on it did
shower;
He kept up a rapid fire, and most accurate,
And when the Austrian commander noticed it he felt irate.

And at sunset the last assault was made.
Still the noble Grenadier felt not the least afraid;
But the Austrian commander sent a second summons of
surrender,
Hoping that the garrison would his injunctions remember.

Then the next day at sunrise the tower door was opened wide,
And a bronzed and scarred Grenadier forth did glide;
Literally laden with muskets, and passed along the line of
troops,
While in utter astonishment the Austrian Colonel upon him
looks.

Behold! Colonel, I am the garrison, said the soldier proudly,
What! exclaimed the Colonel, do you mean to tell me—
That you alone have held that tower against so many men,
Yes! Colonel, I have indeed, replied La Tour d'Auvergne.

Then the Colonel raised his cap and said, you are the bravest
of the brave,
Grenadier, I salute you, and I hope you will find an honourable
grave;
And you're at liberty to carry the muskets along with you,
So my brave Grenadier I must bid thee adieu.

At last in action the brave solider fell in June 1800,
And the Emperor Napoleon felt sorry when he heard he was
    dead;
And he commanded his regiment to remember one thing
    above all,
To cry out always the brave Grenadier's name at the roll call.

TRAGIC DEATH OF
THE REV. A. H. MACKONOCHIE

FRIENDS of humanity, of high and low degree,
I pray ye all come listen to me;
And truly I will relate to ye,
The tragic fate of the Rev. Alexander Heriot Mackonochie

Who was on a visit to the Bishop of Argyle
For the good of his health, for a short while;
Because for the last three years his memory had been affected
Which prevented him from getting his thoughts collected

'Twas on Thursday, the 15th of December, in the year of 1887,
He left the Bishop's house to go and see Loch Leven;
And he was accompanied by a little skye terrier and a
    deerhound,
Besides the Bishop's two dogs, that knew well the ground.

And as he had taken the same walk the day before,
The Bishop's mind was undisturbed and easy on that score
Besides the Bishop had been told by some men,
That they saw him making his way up a glen.

From which a river flows down with a mighty roar,
From the great mountains of the Mamore;
And this route led him towards trackless wastes eastward,
And no doubt to save his life he had struggled very hard.

And as Mr Mackonochie had not returned at dinner time,
The Bishop ordered two men to search for him, which they
    didn't decline;
Then they searched for him along the road he should have
    returned,
But when they found him not, they sadly mourned.

And when the Bishop heard it, he procured a carriage and pair,
While his heart was full of woe, and in a state of despair;
He organised three search parties wihtout delay,
And headed one of the parties in person without dismay.

And each party searched in a different way,
But to their regret at the end of the day;
Most unfortunately no discovery had been made,
Then they lost hope of finding him, and began to be afraid.

And as a last hope, two night searches were planned,
And each party with well lighted lamps in hand
Started on their perilous mission, Mr Mackonochie to try and
    find,
In the midst of driving hail, and the howling wind.

One party searched a distant sporting lodge with right good
    will,
Besides through brier, and bush, and snow, on the hill;
And the Bishop's party explored the Devil's Staircase with
    hearts full of woe,
A steep pass between the Kinloch hills, and the hills of
    Glencoe.

Oh! it was a pitch dark and tempestuous night,
And the searchers would have lost their way without lamp
    light;
But the brave searchers stumbled along for hours, but slow,
Over rocks, and ice, and sometimes through deep snow.

And as the Bishop's party were searching they met a third
     party from Glencoe side,
Who had searched bracken and burn, and the country wide;
And sorrow was depicted in each one's face,
Because of the Rev. Mr Mackonochie they could get no trace

But on Saturday morning the Bishop set off again,
Hoping that the last search wouldn't prove in vain;
Accompanied with a crowd of men and dogs,
All resolved to search the forest and the bogs.

And the party searched with might and main,
Until they began to think their search would prove in vain;
When the Bishop's faithful dogs raised a pitiful cry,
Which was heard by the searchers near by.

Then the party pressed on right manfully,
And sure enough there were the dogs guarding the body of
     Mackonochie;
And the corpse was cold and stiff, having been long dead,
Alas! almost frozen, and a wreath of snow around the head.

And as the searchers gathered round the body in pity they
     did stare,
Because his right foot was stained with blood, and bare;
But when the Bishop o'er the corpse had offered up a prayer,
He ordered his party to carry the corpse to his house on a bier.

So a bier of sticks was most willingly and quickly made,
Then the body was most tenderly upon it laid;
And they bore the corpse and laid inside the Bishop's private
     chapel,
Then the party took one sorrowful look and bade the corpse,
     farewell.

BURNING OF THE STEAMER
"CITY OF MONTREAL"

A sad tale of the sea I will relate, which will your hearts appal,
Concerning the burning of the steamship "City of Montreal,"
Which had on board two hundred and forty-nine souls in all,
But, alas! a fearful catastrophe did them befall.

The steamer left New York on the 6th August with a general
    cargo,
Bound for Queenstown and Liverpool also;
And all went well until Wednesday evening the 10th,
When in an instant an alarming fire was discovered at length.

And most of the passengers had gone to their berths for the
    night,
But when the big bell rang out, oh! what a pitiful sight;
To see mothers and their children crying, was most heart-rending
    to behold,
As the blinding smoke began to ascend from the main hold.

And the smoke before long drifted down below,
Which almost choked the passengers, and filled their hearts
    with woe;
Then fathers and mothers rushed madly upon the deck,
While the crew were struggling manfully the fire to check.

Oh, it was a soul-harrowing and horrible sight,
To see the brave sailors trying hard with all their might;
Battling furiously with the merciless flames —
With a dozen of hose, but still the fire on them gains.

At length it became apparent the steamer couldn't be saved,
And the passengers were huddled together, and some of them
    madly raved;
And the family groups were most touching to see,
Especially husbands and wives embracing each other tenderly.

The mothers drew their little ones close to them,
Just like little lambs huddled together in a pen;
While the white foaming billows was towering mountains high,
And one and all on God for protection did cry.

And when the Captain saw the steamer he couldn't save,
He cried, come men, prepare the boats to be launched onthe
    briny wave;
Be quick, and obey my orders, let each one bear a hand —
And steer the vessel direct for Newfoundland.

Then the men made ready the boats, which were eight on board,
Hurriedly and fearlessly with one accord;
And by eight o'clock on Thursday morning, everything was
    ready
For the passengers to leave the burning steamer that was
    rolling unsteady.

Then Captain Land on his officers loudly did call,
And the cheery manliness of him inspired confidence in all;
Then he ordered the men to lower the boats without delay,
So the boats were launched on the stormy sea without dismay.

Then women and children were first put into them,
Also a quantity of provisions, then followed the men;
And as soon as the boats were loaded they leftthe steamer's
    side,
To be tossed to and fro on the ocean wide.

And just as they left the burning ship, a barque hove in sight,
Which filled the poor creatures hearts with delight;
And the barque was called the "Trebant," of Germany,
So they were all rescued and conveyed to their homes in
    safety.

But before they left the barque, they thanked God that did
  them save
From a cold and merciless watery grave;
Also the Captain received their thanks o'er and o'er,
Whilst the big waves around the barque did sullenly roar.

So good people I warn ye all to be advised by me,
To remember and be prepared to meet God where'er ye may
  be;
For death claims his victims, both on sea and shore,
Therefore be prepared for that happy land where all troubles
  are o'er.

WRECK OF THE WHALER "OSCAR"

'Twas on the 1st of April, and in the year of Eighteen thirteen,
That the whaler "Oscar" was wrecked not far from Aberdeen;
'Twas all on a sudden the wind arose, and a terrific blast it
  blew,
And the "Oscar" was lost, and forty-two of a gallant crew.

The storm burst forth with great violence, but of short
  duration,
And spread o'er a wide district, and filled the people's hearts
  with consternation,
And its effects were such that the people will long mind,
Because at Peterhead the roof was torn off a church by the
  heavy wind.

The "Oscar" joined other four ships that were lying in
  Aberdeen Bay,
All ready to start for Greenland without delay,
While the hearts of each ship' crew felt light and gay,
But, when the storm burst upon them, it filled their hearts
  with dismay.

The wind had been blowing westerly during the night,
But suddenly it shifted to the North-east, and blew with all
   its might,
And thick and fast fell the blinding snow,
Which filled the poor sailors' hearts with woe.

And the "Oscar" was exposed to the full force of the
   gale,
But the crew resolved to do their best, allowing they should
   fail,
So they weighed anchor, and stood boldly out for sea,
While the great crowds that had gathered cheered them
   encouragingly.

The ill-fated "Oscar," however, sent a boat ashore
For some of her crew that were absent, while the angry sea
   did roar,
And 'twas with great difficulty the men got aboard,
And to make the ship alright they wrought with one
   accord.

Then suddenly the wind shifted, and a treacherous calm
   ensued,
And the vessel's deck with snow was thickly strewed;
And a heavy sea was running with a strong flood tide,
And it soon became apparent the men wouldn't be able the
   ship to guide.

And as the "Oscar" drifted further and further to leeward,
The brave crew tried hard her backward drifting to retard,
But all their efforts proved in vain, for the storm broke out
   anew,
While the drifting snow hid her from the spectators'
   view.

And the position of the "Oscar" was critical in the extreme
And as the spray washed o'er the vessel, O what a soul-harrowing
    scene!
And notwithstanding the fury of the gale and the blinding
    snow,
Great crowds watched the "Oscar" as she was tossed to and
    fro.

O heaven! it was a most heart-rending sight
To see the crew struggling against wind and blinding snow
    with all their might,
While the mighty waves lashed her sides and angry did
    roar,
Which to their relatives were painful to see that were
    standing on shore,

All eagerly watching her attempt to ride out the storm,
Especially their friends and relatives, who seemed very forlorn,
Because the scene was awe-inspiring and made them stand
    aghast,
For every moment seemed to be the "Oscar's" last.

Oh! it was horrible to see the good ship in distress,
Battling hard against wind and tide to clear the Girdleness.
A conspicuous promontory on the south side of Aberdeen Bay,
Where many a stout ship and crew have gone down passing
    that way.

At last the vessel was driven ashore in the bay of Greyhope,
And the "Oscar" with the elements no longer could cope.
While the big waves lashed her furiously, and she received
    fearful shocks,
Until a mighty wave hurled her among large boulders of
    rocks.

And when the vessel struck, the crew stood aghast,
But they resolved to hew down the mainmast,
Which the spectators watched with eager interest,
And to make it fall on the rocks the brave sailors tried their
  best.

But, instead of falling on the rocks, it dropped into the angry
  tide,
Then a groan arose from those that were standing on the
  shore side;
And the mainmast in its fall brought down the foremast,
Then all hope of saving the crew seemed gone at last.

And a number of the crew were thrown into the boiling surge
  below,
While loud and angry the stormy wind did blow,
And the good ship was dashed to pieces from stern to stem,
Within a yard or two of their friends, who were powerless to
  save them.

Oh! it was an appalling sight to see the "Oscar" in distress,
While to the forecastle was seen clinging brave Captain Innes
And five of a crew, crying for help, which none could afford,
Alas! poor fellows, crying aloud to God with one accord!

But their cry to God for help proved all in vain,
For the ship and men sank beneath the briny main,
And out of a crew of forty-four men, only two were saved,
But, landsmen, think how manfully that unfortunate crew
  behaved.

And also think of the mariners while you lie down to sleep,
And pray to God to protect them while on the briny deep,
For their hardships are many, and hard to endure,
There's only a plank between them and a watery grave,
  which makes their lives unsure.

JENNY CARRISTER,
THE HEROINE OF LUCKNOW MINE

A heroic story I will unfold,
Concerning Jenny Carrister, a heroine bold,
Who lived in Australia, at a gold mine called Lucknow,
And Jenny was beloved by all the miners, somehow.

Jenny was the only daughter of the old lady who owned the
    mine—
And Jenny would come of an evening, like a gleam of
    sunshine,
And by the presence of her bright face and cheery voice,
She made the hearts of the unlucky diggers rejoice.

There was no pride about her, and day after day,
She walked with her young brother, who was always gay,
A beautiful boy he was, about thirteen years old,
And Jenny and her brother by the miners were greatly extolled.

Old Mrs Carrister was every inch a lady in her way,
Because she never pressed any of the miners that weren't
    able to pay
For the liberty of working the gold-field,
Which was thirty pounds per week for whatever it might yield.

It was in the early part of the year 1871,
That Jack Allingford, a miner, hit on a plan,
That in the mine, with powder, he'd loosen the granite-bound
    face,
So he selected, as he thought, a most suitable place.

And when all his arrangements had been made,
He was lowered down by a miner that felt a little afraid,
But most fortunately Jenny Carrister came up at the time,
Just as Jack Allingford was lowered into the mine.

Then she asked the man at the windlass if he'd had any luck,
But he picked up a piece of candle and then a match he struck;
Then Jenny asked the miner, What is that for?
And he replied to blast the mine, which I fear and abhor.

Then with a piece of rope he lowered the candle and matches
    into the mine,
While brave Jenny watched the action all the time;
And as the man continued to turn round the windlass handle,
Jenny asked him, Isn't it dangerous to lower the matches and
    candle?

Then the man replied, I hope there's no danger, Jenny my lass,
But whatsoever God has ordained will come to pass;
And just as he said so the windlass handle swung round,
And struck him on the forehead, and he fell to the ground.

And when Jenny saw the blood streaming from the fallen
    man's head,
She rushed to the mouth of the shaft without any dread,
And Jenny called loudly, but received no reply,
So to her brother standing near by she heaved a deep sigh.

Telling him to run for assistance, while she swung herself on
    to the hand-rope,
Resolved to save Jack Allingford's life as she earnestly did
    hope;
And as she proceeded down the shaft at a quick pace,
The brave heroine knew that death was staring her in the face.

And the rope was burning her hands as she descended,
But she thought if she saved Jack her task would be ended;
And when she reached the bottom of the mine she did not
    hesitate,
But bounded towards Jack Allingford, who was lying
    seemingly inanimate.

And as she approached his body the hissing fuse burst upon
    her ears,
But still the noble girl no danger fears;
While the hissing of the fuse was like an engine grinding upon
    her brain,
Still she resolved to save Jack while life in her body did remain.

She noticed a small jet of smoke issuing from a hole near his
    head,
And if he'd lain a few seconds longer there he'd been killed dead,
But God had sent an angel to his rescue,
For seizing him by the arms his body to the air shaft she drew.

It was a supernatural effort, but she succeeded at last,
And Jenny thanked God when the danger was past,
But at the same instant the silence was broke
By a loud explosion, which soon filled the mine with smoke.

But, oh, God be thanked! the greatest danger was past,
But when Jenny saw Jack Allingford, she stood aghast,
Because the blood was issuing from his nose and ears,
And as Jenny viewed his wounds she shed many tears.

But heroic Jenny was not one of the fainting sort,
For immediately to the mouth of the mine she did resort,
And she called loudly for help, the noble lass,
And her cry was answered by voices above at the windlass.

So there were plenty to volunteer their services below,
And the rope was attached to the windlass, and down they did
   go,
And Jack Allingford and Jenny were raised to the top,
While Jenny, noble soul, with exhaustion was like to drop.

And when the miners saw her safe above there was a burst of
   applause,
Because she had rescued Jack Allingford from death's jaws;
So all ye that read or hear this story, I have but to say,
That Jenny Carrister was the noblest heroine I've ever heard
   of in my day.

THE HORRORS OF MAJUBA

'Twas after the great Majuba fight:
And the next morning, at daylight,
Captain Macbean's men were ordered to headquarters camp,
So immediately Captain Macbean and his men set out on
   tramp.

And there they were joined by the Blue Jackets and 58th men,
Who, for unflinching courage, no man can them condemn;
And that brave little band was commissioned to bury their
   dead,
And the little band numbered in all about one hundred

And they were supplied with a white flag, fit emblem of death,
Then they started off to O'Neill's farm, with bated breath,
Where their comrades had been left the previous night,
And were lying weltering in their gore, oh! what a horrible
   sight.

And when they arrived at the foot of Majuba Hill,
They were stopped by a Boer party, but they meant no ill,
Who asked them what they wanted without dismay,
And when they said, their dead, there was no further
    delay.

Then the brave heroes marched on, without any dread,
To the Hill of Majuba to collect and bury their dead;
And to see them climbing Majuba it was a fearful sight,
And much more so on a dark pitch night.

And on Majuba there was a row of dead men,
Numbering about forty or fifty of them;
There were also numbers of wounded men lying on the
    ground,
And when Captain Macbean's party gazed on them their
    sorrow was profound.

Oh, heaven! what a sight of blood and brains!
While the grass was red all o'er with blood-stains;
Especially at the edge of the Hill, where the 92nd men were
    killed,
'Twas there that the eyes of Macbean's party with tears filled,

When they saw their dead and dying comrades in arms,
Who were always foremost in the fight during war's alarms;
But who were now lying dead on Majuba Hill,
And, alas! beyond the aid of all human skill.

They then went about two hundred yards down the Hill,
And collected fourteen more bodies, which made their blood
    run chill;
And, into one grave, seventy-five bodies they buried there,
All mostly 92nd men, who, I hope, are free from all care.

Oh! think of that little gallant British band,
Who, at Majuba, made such a heroic stand,
And, take them altogether, they behaved like brave men,
But, alas! they were slaughtered like sheep in a pen.

Poor fellows! there were few of them left to retire,
Because undauntedly they faced that murderous fire,
That the mighty host poured in upon them, left and right,
From their numerous rifles, day and night.

The conduct of the 92nd was most brave throughout,
Which has always been the case, without any doubt;
At least, it has been the case in general with the Highland
    Brigade,
Because in the field they are the foremost, and seldom
    afraid.

And to do the British justice at Majuba they behaved right
    well,
But by overwhelming numbers the most of them fell,
Which I'm very sorry to relate,
That such a brave little band met with such a fate.

The commanders and officers deserve great praise,
Because they told their men to hold Majuba for three days;
And so they did, until the most of them fell,
Fighting nobly for their Queen and country they loved right
    well.

But who's to blame for their fate I'm at a loss to know,
But I think 'twas by fighting too numerous a foe;
But there's one thing I know, and, in conclusion, will say,
That their fame will be handed down to posterity for many
    a day!

MIRACULOUS ESCAPE OF ROBERT ALLAN, THE FIREMAN

'Twas in the year of 1888, and on October the fourteenth
    day,
That a fire broke out in a warehouse, and for hours blazed
    away;
And the warehouse, now destroyed, was occupied by the
    Messrs R. Wylie, Hill & Co.,
Situated in Buchanan Street, in the City of Glasgow.

The flames burst forth about three o'clock in the
    afternoon,
And intimation of the outbreak spread very soon;
And in the spectators' faces were depicted fear and consterna
    tion;
While the news flew like lightning to the Fire Brigade
    Station.

And when the Brigade reached the scene of the fire,
The merciless flames were ascending higher and higher,
Raging furiously in all the floors above the street,
And within twenty minutes the structure was destroyed by
    the burning heat.

Then the roof fell in, pushing out the front wall,
And the loud crash thereof frightened the spectators one and
    all,
Because it shook the neighbouring buildings to their
    foundation,
And caused throughout the City a great sensation

And several men were injured by the falling of the wall,
And as the bystanders gazed thereon, it did their hearts
    appal;
But the poor fellows bore up bravely, without uttering a
    moan,
And with all possible speed they were conveyed home.

The firemen tried to play upon the building where the fire
originated,
But, alas! their efforts were unfortunately frustrated,
Because they were working the hose pipes in a building
occupied by Messrs Smith & Brown,
But the roof was fired, and amongst them it came crashing
    down.

And miraculously they escaped except one fireman,
The hero of the fire, named Robert Allan,
Who was carried with the debris down to the street
    floor,
And what he suffered must have been hard to endure.

He travelled to the fire in Buchanan Street
On the first machine that was ordered, very fleet,
Along with Charles Smith and Dan. Ritchie,
And proceeded to Brown & Smith's buildings that were
    burning furiously.

And in the third floor of the building he took his
    stand
Most manfully, without fear, with the hose in his
    hand,
And played on the fire through a window in the gable
With all his might, the hero, as long as he was able.

And he remained there for about a quarter of an hour,
While from his hose upon the building the water did pour,
When, without the least warning, the floor gave way,
And down he went with it: oh, horror! and dismay!

And with the debris and flooring he got jammed,
But Charlie Smith and Dan. Ritchie quickly planned
To lower down a rope to him, without any doubt,
So, with a long pull and a strong pull, he was dragged
    out.

He thought he was jammed in for a very long time,
For, instead of being only two hours jammed, he thought
    'twas months nine,
But the brave hero kept up his spirits without any dread,
Then he was taken home in a cab, and put in bed.

Oh, kind Christians! think of Robert Allan, the heroic
    man,
For he certainly is a hero, deny it who can?
Because, although he was jammed, and in the midst of the
    flame,
He tells the world fearlessly he felt no pain.

The reason why, good people, he felt no pain
Is because he put his trust in God, to me it seems plain.
And in conclusion, I most earnestly pray,
That we will all put our trust in God, night and day.

And I hope that Robert Allan will do the same,
Because He saved him from being burnt while in the
    flame;
And all those that trust in God will do well,
And be sure to escape the pains of hell.

COLLISION IN THE ENGLISH CHANNEL

'Twas on a Sunday morning, and in the year of 1888,
The steamer "Saxmundham," laden with coal and coke for
    freight,
Was run into amidships by the Norwegian barque
    "Nor,"
And sunk in the English Channel, while the storm fiend did
    roar.

She left Newcastle on Friday, in November, about two
    o'clock,
And proceeded well on her way until she received a
    shock;
And the effects of the collision were so serious within,
That, within twenty minutes afterwards, with water she was
    full to the brim.

The effects of the collision were so serious the water couldn't
    be staunched,
So immediately the "Saxmundham's" jolly-boat was
    launched;
While the brave crew were busy, and loudly did clatter,
Because, at this time, the stem of the steamer was under
    water.

Then the bold crew launched the lifeboat, without dismay,
While their hearts did throb, but not a word did they
    say;
Then they tried to launch the port lifeboat, but in that they
    failed,
Owing to the heavy sea so their sad fate they bewailed.

Then into the jolly-boat and lifeboat jumped fifteen men in all,
And immediately the steamer foundered, which did their
     hearts appal,
As the good ship sank beneath the briny wave,
But they thanked God fervently that did them save.

Oh! it was a miracle how any of them were saved,
But it was by the aid of God, and how the crew behaved;
Because God helps those that help themselves,
And those that don't try to do so are silly elves.

So the two boats cruised about for some time,
Before it was decided to pull for St. Catherine;
And while cruising about they must have been ill,
But they succeeded in picking up an engineer and fireman,
     also Captain Milne.

And at daybreak on Sunday morning the men in the lifeboat
Were picked up by the schooner "Waterbird" as towards
     her they did float,
And landed at Weymouth, and made all right
By the authorities, who felt for them in their sad plight.

But regarding the barque "Nor," to her I must return,
And, no doubt, for the drowned men, many will mourn;
Because the crew's sufferings must have been great,
Which, certainly, is soul-harrowing to relate.

The ill-fated barque was abandoned in a sinking state,
But all her crew were saved, which I'm happy to relate;
They were rescued by the steamer "Hagbrook" in the
     afternoon,
When after taking to their boats, and brought to Portland
     very soon.

The barque "Nor" was bound from New York to Stettin,
And when she struck the "Saxmundham," oh! what a
  terrible din!
Because the merciless water did rush in,
Then the ship carpenters to patch the breach did begin.

But, alas! all their efforts proved in vain,
For still the water did on them gain;
Still they resolved to save her whatever did betide,
But, alas! the ill-fated "Nor" sank beneath the tide.

But thanks be to God, the major part of the men have been
  saved,
And all honour to both crews that so manfully behaved;
And may God protect the mariner by night and by day
When on the briny deep, far, far away!

THE BATTLE OF SHINA, IN AFRICA, FOUGHT IN 1800

King Shuac, the Giant of Mizra, war did declare
Against Ulva, King of Shina, telling him to prepare
And be ready for to meet him in the fight,
Which would commence the next morning before daylight.

When King Ulva heard the news, he told his warriors to
    prepare,
Then suddenly the clatter of arms sounded in the night
    air;
And the pale beams of the moon shone on coats of mail,
But not one bosom beneath them with fear did quail.

And bugles rang out their hoarse call,
And armed men gathered quickly, not in dread of their
    downfall;
For King Ulva resolved to go and meet Shuac,
So, by doing so, King Ulva's men courage didn't lack.

Therefore, the temple was lighted up anew,
And filled with armed warriors, bold and true;
And the King stood clad in his armour, and full of pride,
As he gazed upon his warriors, close by his side.

And he bowed himself to the ground,
While there was a deep silence around;
And he swore, by his false god of the all-seeing eye,
That he would meet Shuac, King of Mizra, and make
    him fly.

And I swear that in Shina peace shall remain,
And whatever thou desireth, supreme one, will not be in vain;
For thou shalt get what thou considereth to be most fit,
Though it be of my own flesh and blood, I swear it.

Then, when all was in readiness, they marched before the dawn,
Sixty thousand in number, and each a picked man;
And they marched on silently to take Shuac's army by
     surprise,
And attack him, if possible, before sunrise.

King Shuac's army were about one hundred thousand strong,
And, when King Ulva heard so, he cried, We'll conquer them
     ere long,
Therefore, march on, brave men, we'll meet them before
     daybreak,
So, be resolute and conquer, and fight for Shina's sake.

Within a mile of the enemy's camp they lay all night,
Scarcely taking well-earned repose, they were so eager for
     the fight;
And when the morning broke clear and cloudless, with a
     burning sun,
Each warrior was wishing that the fight was begun.

And as the armies neared one another, across the fertile land,
It was a most imposing sight, and truly grand,
To see the warriors clad in armour bright,
Especially the form of Shuac, in the midst of the fight.

The royal guard, forming the vanguard, made the first attack,
Under the command of King Ulva, who courage didn't lack;
And cries of "King Ulva!" and "King Shuac!" rent the air,
While Shuac cried, I'll burn Shina to the ground, I now do
     swear!

King Shuac was mounted on a powerful steed,
Which pressed its way through the ranks with lightning
    speed; And with its hoofs the earth it uptears,
Until, with a bound, it dashes through the ranks of opposing
    spears.

Then the two Kings met each other at last,
And fire flashed from their weapons, and blows fell fast;
But Shuac was the strongest of the two,
But King Ulva was his match with the club, Ulva knew.

Then, with his club, he gave Shuac a blow, which wounded
    him deep,
Crying out, Shuac, thy blood is deserting thee! thou art a
    sheep!
Cried Ulva, dealing him another fearful blow,
Then Shuac raised his club and rushed on his foe.

Then his blow fell, and knocked Ulva's club from his hand,
While both armies in amazement stand
To watch the hand-to-hand fight,
While Shuac's warriors felt great delight.

But there chanced to be a Scotchman in Ulva's army
That had a loaded pistol, and he fired it immediately,
And shot King Shuac through the head,
And he toppled over to the ground killed stone dead!

Then the men of Mizra laid down their arms and fled
When they saw that their King was killed dead;
Then King Ulva said to the Scotchman, I am thy servant for
    ever,
For to thee I owe my life, and nought but death will us sever.

BEAUTIFUL EDINBURGH

Beautiful city of Edinburgh, most wonderful to be seen,
With your ancient palace of Holyrood and Queen's Park
   Green,
And your big, magnificent, elegant New College,
Where people from all nations can be taught knowledge.

The New College of Edinburgh is certainly very grand
Which I consider to be an honour to fair Scotland,
Because it's the biggest in the world, without any doubt,
And is most beautiful in the inside as well as out.

And the Castle is wonderful to look upon,
Which has withstood many angry tempests in years
   bygone;
And the rock it's built upon is rugged and lovely to be
   seen
When the shrubberies surrounding it are blown full green.

Morningside is lovely and charming to be seen;
The gardens there are rich with flowers and shrubberies
   green
And sweet scented perfumes fill the air,
Emanating from the sweet flowers and beautiful plants
   there.

And as for Braidhill, it's a very romantic spot,
But a fine place to visit when the weather is hot;
There the air is nice and cool, which will help to drive
   away sorrow
When ye view from its summit the beautiful city of
   Edinburgh.

And as for the statues, they are very grand—
They cannot be surpassed in any foreign land;
And the scenery is attractive and fascinating to the eye,
And arrests the attention of tourists as they pass by.

Lord Melville's Monument is most elegant to be seen,
Which is situated in St. Andrew's Square, amongst
    shrubberies green,
Which seems most gorgeous to the eye,
Because it is towering so very high.

The Prince Albert Consort Statue looks very grand,
Especially the granite blocks whereon it doth stand,
Which is admired by all tourists as they pass by,
Because the big granite blocks seem magnificent to the eye.

Princes Street West End Garden is fascinating to be seen,
With its beautiful big trees and shrubberies green,
And its magnificent water fountain in the valley below
Helps to drive away from the tourist all care and woe.

The Castle Hotel is elegant and grand,
And students visit it from every foreign land,
And the students of Edinburgh often call there
To rest and have luncheon, at a very cheap fare.

Queen Street Garden seems charming to the eye,
And a great boon it is to the tenantry near by,
As they walk along the grand gravel walks near there,
Amongst the big trees and shrubberies, and inhale pure air.

Then, all ye tourists, be advised by me,
Beautiful Edinburgh ye ought to go and see.
It's the only city I know of where ye can wile away the time
By viewing its lovely scenery and statues fine.

Magnificent city of Edinburgh, I must conclude my muse,
But to write in praise of thee I cannot refuse.
I will tell the world boldly without dismay
You have the biggest college in the world at the present
    day.

Of all the cities in the world, Edinburgh for me;
For no matter where I look, some lovely spot I see;
And for picturesque scenery unrivalled you do stand.
Therefore I pronounce you to be the Pride of Fair
    Scotland.

WOMEN'S SUFFRAGE

Fellow men! why should the lords try to despise
And prohibit women from having the benefit of the
    parliamentary Franchise?
When they pay the same taxes as you and me,
I consider they ought to have the same liberty.

And I consider if they are not allowed the same liberty,
From taxation every one of them should be set free;
And if they are not, it is really very unfair,
And an act of injustice I most solemnly declare.

Women, farmers, have no protection as the law now
    stands;
And many of them have lost their property and lands,
And have been turned out of their beautiful farms
By the unjust laws of the land and the sheriffs' alarms.

And in my opinion, such treatment is very cruel;
And fair play, 'tis said, is a precious jewel;
But such treatment causes women to fret and to dote,
Because they are deprived of the parliamentary Franchise
    vote.

In my opinion, what a man pays for he certainly should
    get;
And if he does not, he will certainly fret;
And why wouldn't women do the very same?
Therefore, to demand the parliamentary Franchise they
    are not to blame.

Therefore let them gather, and demand the parliamentary
    Franchise;
And I'm sure no reasonable man will their actions despise,
For trying to obtain the privileges most unjustly withheld
    from them;
Which Mr. Gladstone will certainly encourage and never
    condemn.

And as for the working women, many are driven to the
    point of starvation,
All through the tendency of the legislation;
Besides, upon members of parliament they have no claim
As a deputation, which is a very great shame.

Yes, the Home Secretary of the present day,
Against working women's deputations, has always said—
   nay;
Because they haven't got the parliamentary Franchise,
That is the reason why he does them despise.

And that, in my opinion, is really very unjust;
But the time is not far distant, I most earnestly trust,
When women will have a parliamentary vote,
And many of them, I hope, will wear a better petticoat.

And I hope that God will aid them in this enterprise,
And enable them to obtain the parliamentary Franchise;
And rally together, and make a bold stand,
And demand the parliamentary Franchise throughtout
   Scotland.

And do not rest day nor night—
Because your demands are only right
In the eyes of reasonable men, and God's eyesight;
And Heaven, I'm sure, will defend the right.

Therefore go on brave women! and never fear,
Although your case may seem dark and drear,
And put your trust in God, for He is strong;
And ye will gain the parliamentary Franchise before very.
   long.

LORD ROBERTS' TRIUMPHAL ENTRY INTO PRETORIA

'Twas in the year of 1900, and on the 5th of June,
Lord Roberts entered Pretoria in the afternoon;
His triumphal entry was magnificent to see,
The British Army marching behind him fearlessly.

With their beautiful banners unfurled to the breeze,
But the scene didn't the Boers please;
And they immediately made some show of fight,
But at the charge of the bayonet they were put to fight.

The troops, by the people, were received with loud cheers,
While many of them through joy shed joyous tears;
Because Lord Roberts from bondage had set them free,
Which made them dance and sing with glee.

Lord Roberts' march into Pretoria was inspiring to see,
It is reckoned one of the greatest achievements in our
    military history;
Because the Boers were watching him in front and behind,
But he scattered them like chaff before the wind.

Oh! it was a most beautiful and inspiring sight
To see the British bayonets glittering in the sunlight,
Whilst the bands played "See the conquering hero comes,"
While the people in ecstasy towards them run.

The British marched into Pretoria like the rushing tide,
And the Boers around Pretoria there no longer could abide,
Because the British at the charge of the bayonet made them
    run with fear,
And fly from Pretoria just like wild dear.

Then Lord Roberts cried, "Pull down the Transvaal Flag,
And hoist the Union Jack instead of the Transvaal rag;
And shout 'Britannia for ever,' and 'Long live our Queen,'
For she is the noblest Queen the world has ever seen."

Then the Union Jack was hoisted and unfurled to the breeze,
Which certainly did the Boers displease,
When they saw the Union Jack flying o'er their capital,
The sight thereof amazed them, and did them appall.

And when old Kruger saw Lord Roberts he shook with
    fright,
Then he immediately disguised himself and took to flight,
Leaving his poor wife in Pretoria behind,
But the British troops have treated her very kind.

Now let us all thank Lord Roberts for his great bravery,
Who has gained for the people of Pretoria their liberty,
By his skillful tactics and great generalship, be it told,
And the courage of his soldiers, who fought like lions bold.

Lord Roberts is a brave man, be it said,
Who never was the least afraid
To defend his Queen and country when called upon;
And by his valorous deeds great battles he has won.

Then success to Lord Roberts and the British Army,
May God protect them by land and by sea;
And enable them always to conquer the Boers,
And beat all foreign foes from our shores.

TRIBUTE TO MR J. GRAHAM HENDERSON, THE WORLD'S FAIR JUDGE

Thrice welcome home to Hawick, Mr J. Graham Henderson,
For by your Scotch tweeds a great honour you have won;
By exhibiting your beautiful tweeds at the World's Fair
You have been elected judge of Australian and American
    wools while there.

143

You had to pass a strict examination on the wool trade,
But you have been victorious, and not the least afraid,
And has been made judge of wools by Sir Henry Truman
    Good,
And was thanked by Sir Henry where he stood.

You have been asked by Sir Henry to lecture on wools
    there,
And you have consented to do so, which made your
    audience stare
When you let them see the difference betwixt good wool
    and bad;
You'll be sure to gain fresh honours, they will feel so glad.

To think they have found a clever man indeed,
That knows good wool and how to manufacture Scotch
    tweed,
I wish you success for many a long day,
Because your Scotch tweeds are the best, I venture to say.

May you always be prosperous wherever you go,
Always gaining fresh friends, but never a foe,
Because you are good and a very clever man,
And to gainsay it there's few people can.

WRECK OF THE COLUMBINE

Kind Christians, all pay attention to me,
And Miss Mouat's sufferings I'll relate to ye;
While on board the Columbine, on the merciless sea;
Tossing about in the darkness of night in the storm
    helplessly.

She left her home (Scatness), on Saturday morning, bound
    for Lerwick,
Thinking to get cured by a man she knew, as she was very
    sick;
But for eight days she was tossed about on the stormy main,
By a severe storm of wind, hail, and rain.

The waves washed o'er the little craft, and the wind
    loudly roared,
And the Skipper, by a big wave, was washed overboard;
Then the crew launched the small boat on the stormy
    main,
Thinking to rescue the Skipper, but it was all in vain.

Nevertheless, the crew struggled hard his life to save,
But alas! the Skipper sank, and found a watery grave;
And the white crested waves madly did roar,
Still the crew, thank God, landed safe on shore.

As soon as Miss Mouat found she was alone,
Her mind became absorbed about her friends at home;
As her terrible situation presented itself to her mind,
And her native place being quickly left far behind.

And as the big waves lashed the deck with fearful shocks,
Miss Mouat thought the vessel had struck upon a reef of
    rocks;
And she thought the crew had gone to get help from land,
While she held to a rope fastened to the cabin roof by her
    right hand.

And there the poor creature was in danger of being thrown
    to the floor,
Whilst the heavy showers of spray were blown against the
    cabin door,
And the loosened sail was reduced to tatters and flapping
    with the wind,
And the noise thereof caused strange fears to arise in her
    mind.

And after some hours of darkness had set in,
The table capsized with a lurch of the sea which made a
    fearful din,
Which helped to put the poor creature in a terrible fright,
To hear the drawers of the table rolling about all the night.

And there the noble heroine sat looking very woe-begone,
With hands uplifted to God making her moan,
Praying to God above to send her relief,
While in frantic screams she gave vent to her pent up grief.

And loud and earnestly to God the noble heroine did cry,
And the poor invalid's bosom heaved many a sigh;
Oh! heaven, hard was the fate of this woman of sixty years
    of age,
Tossing about on the briny deep, while the storm fiend did
    rage.

Oh! think of the poor soul crouched in the cabin below,
With her heart full of fear, cold, hunger, and woe,
And the pitless storm of rain, hail, and snow,
Tossing about her tiny craft to and fro.

And when the morning came she felt very sick,
And she expected the voyage would be about three hours
    to Lerwick,
And her stock of provisions was but very small,
Only two half-penny biscuits and a quart bottle of milk in
    all

Still the heavy snow kept falling, and the sky was
    obscured,
And on Sabbath morning she made her first meal on
    board,
And this she confined to a little drop of milk and half a
    biscuit,
Which she wisely considered was most fit.

And to the rope fastened to the cabin roof she still held on
Until her hands began to blister, and she felt woe-begone,
But by standing on a chest she could look out of the
    hatchway,
And spend a little time in casting her eyes o'er the sea
    each day.

When Wednesday morning came the weather was very
    fine,
And the sun in the heavens brightly did shine,
And continued so all the live long day;
Then Miss Mouat guessed that land to the norward lay.

Then the poor creature sat down to her last meal on board,
And with heartfelt thanks she praised the Lord;
But when Thursday morning came no more food could be
    had,
Then she mounted a box about seven o'clock while her heart
    felt sad.

147

And she took her usual gaze o'er the sea with a wistful eye,
Hoping that some passing vessel she might descry,
And to the westward she espied a bright red light,
But as the little craft passed on it vanished from her sight.

But alas; no vessel could she see around anywhere,
And at last the poor soul began to despair,
And there the lonely woman sat looking out to the heavens
   above,
Praying to God for succour with her heart full of love.

At last the Columbine began to strike on submerged rocks,
And with the rise and fall of the sea she received some
   dreadful shocks,
And notwithstanding that the vessel was still rolling
   among the rocks,
Still the noble heroine contrived once more to raise herself
   upon the box.

Still the Columbine sped on, and ran upon a shingly
   beach,
And at last the Island of Lepsoe, Miss Mouat did reach,
And she was kindly treated by the inhabitants in everyway
   that's grand,
And conveyed to Aalesund and there taking steamer to fair
   England.

BALMORAL CASTLE

Beautiful Balmoral Castle,
   Most handsome to be seen,
Highland home of the Empress of India,
   Great Britain's Queen.

Your woods and waters and
  Mountains high are most
Beautiful to see,
  Near by Balmoral Castle
And the dark river Dee.

Then there's the hill of Cairngorm
  To be seen from afar,
And the beautiful heathery hills
  Of dark Lochnagar,
And the handsome little village—
  The Castleton o'Braemar—
Which is most beautiful to see,
  Near by Balmoral Castle
And the dark river Dee.

Then there's the handsome little church
  Of Crathie — most beautiful to be seen;
And the Queen goes there on Sunday
  To hear the Word of God
Most solemn and serene,
  Which is most beautiful to see,
Nor far from Balmoral Castle
  And the dark river Dee.

Then, when she finds herself
  At leisure, she goes for to see
Her old female acquaintances
  That lives on the river Dee,
And reads the Bible unto them,
  Which is most beautiful to see,
Near by Balmoral Castle
  And the dark river Dee.

Beautiful Balmoral Castle!
　In the summer season of the year
The Queen comes to reside in thee,
　Her spirits for to cheer,
And to see her hiland deer,
　And in the green woods to roam
And admire the hiland cataracts,
　With their misty foam,
Which is most beautiful to see,
　Near by Balmoral Castle
And the dark river Dee.

Beautiful Balmoral Castle,
　With your green swards and flowers fair,
Thee Queen of great Britain
　Is always welcome there;
For they young and they old
　Tries to do for her all they can,
And they faithful Highlanders there
　Will protect her to a man,
Which is most beautiful to see,
　Near by Balmoral Castle
And thee dark river Dee.

A NEW TEMPERANCE POEM, IN MEMORY OF MY DEPARTED PARENTS, WHO WERE SOBER LIVING & GODFEARING PEOPLE

My parents were sober living, and often did pray,
For their family to abstain from intoxicating drink alway;
Because they knew it would lead them astray,
Which no God fearing man will dare to gainsay.

Some people do say that God made strong drink,
But he is not so cruel I think;
To lay a stumbling block in his children's way,
And then punish them for going astray.

No! God has more love for his children, than mere man.
To make strong drink their souls to damn;
His love is more boundless than mere man's by far,
And to say not it would be an unequal par.

A man that truly loves his family wont allow them to
    drink,
Because he knows seldom about God they will think,
Besides he knows it will destroy their intellect,
And cause them to hold their parents in disrespect.

Strong drink makes the people commit all sorts of evil,
And must have been made by the Devil
For to make them quarrel, murder, steal, and fight,
And prevent them from doing what is right.

The Devil delights in leading the people astray,
So that he may fill his kingdom with them without delay;
It is the greatest pleasure he can really find,
To be the enemy of all mankind.

The Devil delights in breeding family strife,
Especially betwixt man and wife;
And if the husband comes home drunk at night,
He laughs and crys, ha! ha! what a beautiful sight.

And if the husband asks his supper when he comes in,
The poor wife must instantly find it for him;
And if she cannot find it, he will curse and frown,
And very likely knock his loving wife down.

Then the children will scream aloud,
And the Devil no doubt will feel very proud,
If he can get the children to leave their own fireside,
And to tell their drunken father, they won't with him
    reside.

Strong drink will cause the gambler to rob and kill his
    brother,
Aye! also his father and his mother,
All for the sake of getting money to gamble,
Likewise to drink, cheat, and wrangle.

And when the burglar wants to do his work very handy,
He plies himself with a glass of Whisky, Rum, or Brandy,
To give himself courage to rob and kill,
And innocent people's blood to spill.

Whereas if the couldn't get Whisky, Rum, or Brandy,
He wouldn't do his work so handy;
Therefore, in that respect let strong drink be abolished in
    time,
And that will cause a great decrease in crime.

Therefore, for this sufficient reason remove it from
    society,
For seldom burglary is committed in a state of sobriety;
And I earnestly entreat ye all to join with heart and hand,
And to help to chase away the Demon drink from bonnie
    Scotland.

I beseech ye all to kneel down and pray,
And implore God to take it away;
Then this world would be a heaven, whereas it is a hell,
And the people would have more peace in it to dwell.

THE SUNDERLAND CALAMITY

'Twas in the town of Sunderland, and in the year of 1883,
That about 200 children were launch'd into eternity
While witnessing an entertainment in Victoria Hall,
While they, poor little innocents, to God for help did call.

The entertainment consisted of conjuring, and the ghost
    illusion play,
Also talking waxworks, and living marionettes, and given
    by Mr Fay;
And on this occasion, presents were to be given away,
But in their anxiety of getting presents they wouldn't
    brook delay,
And that is the reason why so many lives have been taken
    away;
But I hope their precious souls are in heaven to-day.

As soon as the children began to suspect
That they would lose their presents by neglect,
They rush'd from the gallery, and ran down the stairs
    pell-mell,
And trampled one another to death, according as they fell.

As soon as the catastrophe became known throughout the
boro'
The people's hearts were brim-full of sorrow,
And parents rush'd to the Hall terror-stricken and wild,
And each one was anxious to find their own child.

Oh! it must have been a most horrible sight
To see the dear little children struggling with all their
might
To get out at the door at the foot of the stair,
While one brave little boy did repeat the Lord's Prayer.

The innocent children were buried seven or eight layers
deep,
The sight was heart-rending and enough to make one weep;
It was a most affecting spectacle and frightful to behold
The corpse of a little boy not above four years old,

Who had on a top-coat much too big for him,
And his little innocent face was white and grim,
And appearing to be simply in a calm sleep —
The sight was enough to make one's flesh to creep.

The scene in the Hall was heart-sickening to behold,
And enough to make one's blood run cold.
To see the children's faces, blackened, that were trampled
to death,
And their parents lamenting o'er them with bated breath.

Oh! it was most lamentable for to hear
The cries of the mothers for their children dear;
And many mothers swooned in grief away
At the sight of their dead children in grim array.

154

There was a parent took home a boy by mistake,
And after arriving there his heart was like to break
When it was found to be the body of a neighbour's child;
The parent stood aghast and was like to go wild.

A man and his wife rush'd madly in the Hall,
And loudly in grief on their children they did call,
And the man searched for his children among the dead
Seemingly without the least fear or dread.

And with his finger pointing he cried. "That's one! two!
Oh! heaven above, what shall I do;"
And still he kept walking on and murmuring very low.
Until he came to the last child in the row;

Then he cried, "Good God! all my family gone
And now I am left to mourn alone;"
And staggering back he cried, "Give me water, give me
    water!"
While his heart was like to break and his teeth seem'd to
    chatter.

Oh, heaven! it must have been most pitiful to see
Fathers with their dead children upon their knee
While the blood ran copiously from their mouths and ears
And their parents shedding o'er them hot burning tears.

I hope the Lord will comfort their parents by night and by
    day,
For He gives us life and He takes it away,
Therefore I hope their parents will put their trust in Him,
Because to weep for the dead it is a sin.

Her Majesty's grief for the bereaved parents has been
   profound,
And I'm glad to see that she has sent them£50;
And I hope from all parts of the world will flow relief
To aid and comfort the bereaved parents in their grief.

INAUGURATION OF THE UNIVERSITY COLLEGE, DUNDEE

Good people of Dundee, your voices raise,
And to Miss Baxter give great praise;
Rejoice and sing and dance with glee,
Because she has founded a College in Bonnie Dundee.

Therefore loudly in her praise sing,
And make Dundee with your voices ring,
And give honour to whom honour is due,
Because ladies like her are very few.

'Twas on the 5th day of October, in the year of 1883,
That the University College was opened in Dundee,
And the opening proceedings were conducted in the College
   Hall,
In the presence of ladies and gentlemen both great and small.

Worthy Provost Moncur presided over the meeting,
And received very great greeting;
And Professor Stuart made an eloquent speech there,
And also Lord Dalhousie, I do declare.

Also, the Right Hon W.E. baxter was there on behalf of
    his aunt,
And acknowledged her beautiful portrait without any rant,
And said that she requested him to hand it over to the
    College,
As an incentive to others to teach the ignorant masses
    knowledge,

Success to Miss Baxter, and praise to the late Doctor Baxter,
    John Boyd,
For I think the Dundonians ought to feel overjoyed
For their munificent gifts to the town of Dundee,
Which will cause their names to be handed down to
    posterity.

The College is most handsome and magnificent to be seen,
And Dundee can now almost cope with Edinburgh or
    Aberdeen,
For the ladies of Dundee can now learn useful knowledge
By going to their own beautiful College.

I hope the ladies and gentlemen of Dundee will try and
    learn knowledge
At home in Dundee in their nice little College,
Because knowledge is sweeter than honey or jam,
Therefore let them try and gain knowledge as quick as they
    can.

It certainly is a great boon and an honour to Dundee
To have a College in our midst, which is most charming to
    see,
All through Miss Baxter and the late Dr Baxter, John Boyd,
Which I hope by the people of Dundee will long be enjoyed.

Now since Miss Baxter has lived to see it erected,
I hope by the students she will long be respected
For establishing a College in Bonnie Dundee,
where learning can be got of a very high degree.

"My son, get knowledge," so said the sage,
For it will benefit you in your old age,
And help you through this busy world to pass,
For remember a man without knowledge is just like an ass.

I wish the Professors and teachers every success,
Hoping the Lord will all their labours bless;
And I hope the students will always be obedient to their
    teachers,
And that many of them may learn to be orators and
    preachers.

I hope Miss Baxter will prosper for many a long day
For the money that she has given away,
May God shower his blessings on her wise head,
And may all good angels guard her while liging and
    hereafter when dead.